Entrepreneurship

A PRIMER

EAMONN BUTLER

AMERICAN INSTITUTE FOR ECONOMIC RESEARCH

Entrepreneurship: A Primer

Written by Eamonn Butler

ISBN: 9781630692063

Cover art: Vanessa Mendozzi

EAMONN BUTLER

Entrepreneurship

A PRIMER

AIER | AMERICAN INSTITUTE *for* ECONOMIC RESEARCH

Contents

1

Introduction

What this book is about

This is not a management book about how to make yourself a successful entrepreneur. It is a basic introduction to what entrepreneurship is, why we need it, and how we can encourage it.

Accordingly, the book explains what is distinctive and important about entrepreneurship and its role in boosting innovation, progress, productivity and economic growth. That is important, because these crucial contributions of entrepreneurship are not widely understood. Indeed, they are often completely overlooked in mainstream economics textbooks. Yet they make entrepreneurship vital to all of us as workers, consumers and citizens.

Who this book is for

Certainly, business managers may well find value in this book in terms of putting what they do into the wider economic, institutional and policy context. But the book's main audience is ordinary people who want to understand the role of innovation and entrepreneurship in driving economic progress, and students who find the standard textbook on economics mechanistic, sterile and lacking any human reality.

> *"If I had asked people what they wanted, they would have said faster horses."*
>
> **—Henry Ford, American carmaker**

It should also be of value to readers in developing countries who want to make their economies less centralised and more free, open, diverse, dynamic, productive and prosperous. In developed countries, the book should be useful to those who are involved in public policy but who do not fully understand the role and importance of entrepreneurship in economic life.

Entrepreneurship and the author

I have seen visionary entrepreneurs give people new opportunities and change their lives. In the 1970s, Freddy Laker's *Skytrain* broke the old airline cartel and enabled millions of us to cross the Atlantic affordably—and to bring back new ideas as we did so. Clive Sinclair developed the pocket calculator and digital watch. The Sony Corporation created the Walkman portable music player. Bill Gates brought computers into our homes. Tim Berners-Lee linked us all to the world's knowledge through the Web. And Steve Jobs's iPhone put all these things, plus much else, into the pockets of two billion people. (Well, not the airline, but certainly the whole world's transport schedules and booking apps.)

Few entrepreneurs are household names, though. To some extent, we are *all* entrepreneurs. As a new graduate, for example, I took the opportunity to migrate and escape recession in my home country.

I returned to set up a non-profit policy group at a time when new ideas were sorely needed. Now, I am trying to fill another niche by writing primers like this one. I am no businessperson, but I still act entrepreneurially.

> *"Being an entrepreneur simply means being someone who wants to make a difference to other people's lives."*
>
> **—Sir Richard Branson, founder, Virgin Group**

Mainstream economics teaching imagines the economy as a mechanism that can be predicted and controlled. Experience taught me just how far this image is from reality. Real economic life is about *people* and the relationships between them. It is motivated by their aims and actions. Their entrepreneurship is what boosts human prosperity and progress. But entrepreneurship's role is overlooked in mainstream thinking—and then unwittingly smothered by bad public policy based on that view.

We need to rehabilitate entrepreneurship into mainstream economics and politics. All over the world, there are courses in art, music or film appreciation. We need to appreciate the contribution of entrepreneurship to our lives as well.

Structure of the book

This book is a small contribution to that appreciation. First, it explains why we should care about entrepreneurship—what it means to innovation and prosperity, and how we might encourage it. It then looks at how we commonly talk about entrepreneurship and tries to draw out what the core idea actually is, and what really motivates entrepreneurs.

The fourth chapter examines different theories of the true economic role of entrepreneurship, while the next two explore its economic and social importance and its amazing prevalence throughout the world and in different industries.

Chapter 7 reveals that not all entrepreneurship is productive. It can even be damaging if it becomes focused on manipulating regulations rather than serving customers. Chapter 8 asks whether governments encourage entrepreneurship to develop. The answer is maybe, but too often they get it completely wrong. They forget that entrepreneurship thrives only within an open and competitive economy. The book concludes by describing the policy environment we must create if we are to reap the benefits of entrepreneurship and not kill it stone dead.

2

Why care about entrepreneurship?

The unseen factor of production

Entrepreneurship is more important to us than we think. Most of us realise that land, labour and capital are needed in order to produce the goods and services that sustain and improve our lives. But entrepreneurship is the *unseen* factor of production. Land, labour and capital produce nothing until they are actively put to work. They need to be directed and focused by some human mind—an *entrepreneurial* mind that realises how they can be used to create value.

> *"Classical economics established four fundamental factors of production: land, labor, capital, and entrepreneurship.... With a few exceptions, the last factor disappeared, along with purposeful action, from economic theory sometime around the beginning of the 20th century."*

—Frédéric Sautet, in Peter Boettke,
Israel M Kirzner on Competitive Behavior, Industrial Structure, and the Entrepreneurial Market Process

Indeed, entrepreneurship is so overlooked that even the concept of it is comparatively recent. The word's roots lie in the13th century French *entreprendre*, meaning to do or undertake something. By the 16th century it was being applied to people running businesses. But it was not until 1730 that the Irish-French economist Richard Cantillon (c.1680-1734) used it for someone who took a *financial risk* in running a business; and 1803 when the French economist Jean-Baptiste Say (1767-1832) explained the key role of entrepreneurs in finding *more productive uses* for resources.

Further embellishment of the idea came in 1848, when the British philosopher and economist John Stuart Mill (1806-1873) identified entrepreneurs as people who assume *both the risk and the management* of a business. Today, economists focus on the role of entrepreneurs as *innovators* or in *spotting opportunities* or taking risks in a world of future *uncertainty*. And attempts to clarify the concept continue.

Innovation and economic growth

None of these aspects of entrepreneurship is more important to human progress and economic growth than *innovation*. Progress and growth are not simply the result of applying more of the *seen* factors of production but are largely the result of innovation in making human economic activity more productive. In a competitive economy, entrepreneurs face constant pressure to innovate as they strive to find ever-more cost-effective ways to create the cheaper, better, faster, neater, smarter products that will attract customers. (Just think of the developments in phone or automobile technology, for example, and the revolutions in how they are manufactured.) That constant pressure to raise productivity—finding more efficient processes and more effective products—explains most of the rise in our living standards. Indeed, back in the 1950s, the

American Nobel economist Robert Solow (1924-) calculated that a remarkable 87% of economic growth came from innovation.[1] Yet the British science writer Matt Ridley (1958-) believes the figure is even higher today, since new materials, new machines and more efficient methods allow us to spend less and less time and resources on supplying our needs and wants.[2]

Innovation does not just create better products, it creates new resources too, says the American management expert Peter Drucker (1909-).[3] Entrepreneurs change valueless things like sand into valuable ones like silicon computer chips. And in turn those new resources can be used to create things of even greater value, such as smartphones, robots and driverless cars.

But innovation is not just about new gadgets. It is, says Ridley, "the great equaliser." Today, people in the poorest countries have mobile phones that work as well as any in the richest. Innovation is why the number of people living in extreme poverty is shrinking fast, and why it will continue to do so.[4]

Innovation, then, improves our lives; and there is a powerful link between innovation and the number of new businesses being created. Fast-growing industries (such as IT, AI, VR, biotech, telehealth, fintech) are mostly populated by young, growing firms, not old established

....

1 Solow, R. (1956) 'A Contribution to the Theory of Economic Growth'. In *The Quarterly Journal of Economics,* 70(1) 65-94.

2 Ridley, M. (2020) *How Innovation Works*. Fourth Estate.

3 Drucker, P. (1985) *Innovation and Entrepreneurship*. Butterworth-Heineman.

4 Ridley (2020)

ones.[5] Certainly, large firms, with their capital and personnel resources, can be entrepreneurial too: remember the Sony Walkman. But it is new, smaller, growing companies that account for most innovation, and most new job creation.

How to promote entrepreneurship?

Some Westerners worry that their entrepreneurial business dynamism is declining. The rate of new start-ups has slowed, less productive firms are surviving longer, and the most productive firms are employing more technology and fewer people.[6] Given the economic importance of entrepreneurs in boosting productivity through new products and processes, and their social importance in improving all our lives, this opens up a crucial question: are Western policymakers still maintaining the right conditions for entrepreneurship to thrive, and what must they do to encourage it?

Unfortunately, there are no easy answers. There are few hard facts to go on because 'entrepreneurship' is difficult to define and identify. It might be found mostly in new small companies, but the number of new small businesses in a country is not a good measure of entrepreneurship. After all, there are lots of self-employed house painters or taxi drivers, but they are not normally regarded as *entrepreneurs*. That term is reserved for more dynamic and creative people who re-organise production methods and produce something new. As Peter Drucker put

5 Sanandaji, T. and Sanandaji, N. (2014) 'SuperEntrepreneurs—And how your country can get them.' London: Centre for Policy Studies.

6 Decker, R. A., J. Haltiwanger, R. S. Jarmin and J. Miranda (2016) 'Declining Business Dynamism: Implications for Productivity?' *Brookings Institution*, Hutchins Centre Working Paper No. 23, September 19.

it, there are plenty of small restaurants in American suburbs. But the McDonald's owner Ray Kroc standardised the product, revolutionised the process of making it, and created a new market: that is why he is regarded as an entrepreneur.[7]

> *"The husband and wife who open another delicatessen store or another Mexican restaurant in the American suburb surely take a risk. But are they entrepreneurs? All they do is what has been done many times before.... But by applying management concepts and management techniques (asking, What is 'value' to the customer?), standardizing the 'product,' designing process and tools, and by basing training on the analysis of the work to be done and then setting the standards it required, McDonald's both drastically upgraded the yield from resources, and created a new market and a new customer. This is entrepreneurship."*
>
> **—Peter F. Drucker, *Innovation and Entrepreneurship***

Policymakers might aim to boost entrepreneurship by giving subsidies and other aid to all new businesses. That may well help the few entrepreneurs to flourish, but it would waste taxpayers' money on supporting many other new businesses that are not really entrepreneurial at all. Moreover, most new businesses fail. Typically, a fifth of new businesses fail within one year, a third within two years, and

7 Drucker (1985).

around half within five.[8] Only a tiny few become hugely successful. The rest fail for many and diverse reasons that may have nothing to do with how entrepreneurial or not they are, or how innovative and useful their products might be. If taxpayers' money is used to subsidise all new businesses, it will benefit few successes and be lost on many failures. And sadly, there is no certain way of predicting which new businesses will prosper—which is why governments' attempts to 'pick winners' have usually failed too.

Encouraging experimentation

A better strategy, say some economists, is to try to create the right *conditions* under which entrepreneurship might arise and thrive.[9] The *entrepreneurial process*, by which innovative companies and products either fail or break through to economic success, is an *evolutionary process*, much like the natural selection process by which living species evolve. The more *experimentation* we can encourage, the greater chance we have of finding success. And for the same 'trial and error' reason, the easier it is to *fail*—but still recover—the more fertile the process becomes. Indeed, most successful entrepreneurs have had past failures, often many of them. Thomas Edison had more than a thousand failed attempts to develop a lightbulb. Steve Jobs lost Apple millions with his Apple I and Apple Lisa, and even got fired from his own company. Sir James Dyson tried over five thousand prototypes before creating

8 US Small Business Administration Office of Advocacy, (2014) *New Business Statistics 2004-14.*

9 See, for example, Lerner, J. (2009) *Boulevard of Broken Dreams: Why Public Efforts to Boost Entrepreneurship and Venture Capital Have Failed—And What to Do about it.* Princeton University Press.

his bagless vacuum cleaner. Peter Thiel ran a hedge fund, which lost 95% of its assets.[10] When Amazon branched out from books to toys, Jeff Bezos bought tens of millions of toys to stock, but sold only half of them. Failure teaches entrepreneurs what sorts of processes and products *do not* work, and through their past experience they learn what the market *does* want. Bezos's online auction site failed too—but the experience enabled him to develop Amazon Marketplace.

"I have not failed. I've just found 10,000 ways that won't work."

—Thomas Edison

While there is some science to encouraging entrepreneurship, there is a great deal of guesswork too. Silicon Valley—nickname of the southern San Francisco Bay Area that is home to some of the world's biggest high-tech companies and thousands of tech start-ups—is a celebrated entrepreneurial success story. But few if any places have been able to emulate it, and nobody is quite sure how it came about. Experts argue over whether it was built on public or private investment. The presence of strong 'anchor' firms, many servicing public infrastructure and defence contracts, certainly helped.[11] But then the proximity of Stanford University, a private institution, was also critical. The area also

....

10 Wikipedia (2020) 'Clarium Capital'.

11 Mazzucato, M. (2013) *The Entrepreneurial State*. London: Anthem Press.

benefited from being able to attract mobile, highly educated and skilled workers, and from a thriving local business environment including venture capitalists from whom start-ups could obtain both funding and advice. Then the whole 'clustering' effect of similar tech firms entering the area helped create valuable cross-fertilisation between different companies and increased the specialisation that was available in the jobs market. It was, perhaps, all a lucky accident, which other places would struggle to recreate.

How economists neglect entrepreneurship

Mainstream economists, however, can give us scant guidance on how to boost the entrepreneurial process, because they almost entirely overlook it.

Entrepreneurship is crucial to us all as the driver of economic growth and prosperity. It motivates, directs and organises the other factors of production into the creation of value. Yet mainstream economists rarely appreciate this important catalytic function. In the mainstream economics textbooks, for example, the 'firm' is an entirely abstract idea. There are no explanations of why firms exist, how they are born, how different and diverse they are (apart perhaps from size), how they change and develop, what they mean to their founders, workers and customers—or even why they fail. In other words, human beings and entrepreneurial minds are entirely painted out of the picture. But human beings in general and entrepreneurs in particular are the key to understanding all economic life. It is they who motivate action, commerce and trade. Land, capital and even labour produce nothing of value until they are directed by some human mind to some purposive end. Sand is just sand, until human beings make it into concrete or computer chips; capital goods are just idle equipment until put to work on producing things of value; digging ditches is wasted effort unless it helps us drain or irrigate farmland or provide the footings for buildings or serve some other human purpose. Before we can understand economics, we must understand human motives and interactions.

Sadly, it is much easier for people to comprehend a simple 'mechanical' model of the economy than such richly complex human explanations. The easy textbook concepts such as 'perfect markets'—an imaginary world of identical products and identical buyers and sellers for whom trade is free and costless—are simpler to grasp than the swirling change and diversity of real markets. But those concepts are sterile and unreal.

Even more unfortunately, the 'perfect markets' idea suggests that wherever we find real markets to be 'imperfect', we (or specifically our government policymakers) should immediately intervene and try to bring them back to 'perfection'. But markets are not and never can be 'perfect'. If our economic life was perfect, nobody would have any reason to innovate or supply or sell or buy any produce, because they could never improve things. No *market* would be needed; no market would exist at all. In reality, it is the very *imperfections* in economic life that cause people to take productive action and to trade things between each other. And tomorrow, circumstances will be different again. Markets respond to those changing circumstances. They are dynamic—a perpetual flux of changing demand for and supply of countless goods and services. That flux itself exposes other surpluses, shortages and opportunities just like the whirlpools and eddies that open up in a fast-flowing mountain stream. It is entrepreneurs who take action to fill those eddies with new processes and products. To do so, they innovate. And by innovating, they bring people new goods, services and choices that they might not even have imagined just a short time before.

Entrepreneurs do all this, even without the 'perfect information' that the textbooks imagine. They cannot know in advance which processes will prove practicable and profitable, nor what products the public might want, of what quality and at what price. Their task is all guesswork—albeit, in the case of many successful entrepreneurs, inspired and thoughtful guesswork. Entrepreneurs take risks, make investment decisions, and commit time, effort, capital and other resources into their project, while facing a fog of uncertainty about what the future will bring and what the needs and choices of future consumers will be. Who would have dreamed, for example, that nearly half the world's population would even want a smartphone, never mind buy one? What producer of encyclopaedias, atlases, reference books, diaries, newspapers, calculating machines, cameras, music players or department stores would have predicted that their businesses would be devastated by some pocket gadget? But taking risks against such a background of uncertainty is, according to some theorists, the very definition of entrepreneurism.[12]

The importance of competition

The textbook view also suggests that competition is a *state of affairs*—a fixed situation in which there are large numbers of identical buyers and sellers. But as the Anglo-Austrian Nobel economist F. A. Hayek (1899-1992) realised, competition is better thought of as an active and ongoing *process*. Moreover, it is a process in which entrepreneurs and

....

12 McMaken, R. (2014) 'Extended Version of Peter Klein's Interview on Entrepreneurship.' *Mises Institute*, Mises Wire, April 8.

entrepreneurship play a vital part.[13]

Hayek called competition a *discovery procedure*. As entrepreneurs juggle with the changing demands of customers and variations in the price and supply of resources, they discover new information. They find better and cheaper ways of producing goods and services, and identify the needs, wants and tastes of customers more precisely.

Under the pressure of competition, there is also a premium on entrepreneurs satisfying those desires as quickly as possible. Surpluses, shortages and opportunities occur all the time in markets—a natural result of their dynamism and complexity, and the daily fluctuations and mismatches in supply, demand and prices that inevitably open up. Entrepreneurs are rewarded for acting to stem the surpluses, plug the shortages and seize the opportunities that occur—and for anticipating future surpluses and shortages and acting in advance to correct them. Under market competition, entrepreneurs must act fast, or competitors will gladly exploit those opportunities and gain the rewards of success instead. In a competitive market, therefore, mismatches are corrected quickly, far quicker than could happen if the market was governed by government planners or dominated by monopolists, neither of whom would have such an urgent interest in doing so. The greater the competition, the faster must entrepreneurs be in spotting and plugging gaps, the more accurate they must become in anticipating future demands, and the more innovative and imaginative they must be in correcting imbalances. The more rapidly they serve the true needs of the public, and the better they are at it, the more their actions make the whole society better off.

....

13 Hayek, F. (1978) 'Competition as a Discovery Procedure'. In *New Studies in Philosophy, Politics, Economics and the History of Ideas*. London: Routledge & Kegan Paul.

"Nobody talks of entrepreneurship as survival, but that's exactly what it is and what nurtures creative thinking."

—Anita Roddick, founder of BodyShop

Again, competition can be seen as an evolutionary process of *selection*. But it is not *producers*, not businesses and entrepreneurs, who select what products we will have. It is *consumers*, constantly choosing the products that best satisfy their needs and give them the highest value for the least price. If someone else can produce a better or cheaper product that delivers them better value for money, they can (and generally will) drop their existing suppliers and spend their money on that new product and new supplier instead. Build a better mousetrap, as the saying goes, and the world will beat a path to your door—though there is much more to entrepreneurial success than mere invention.

Through the competitive market selection process, resources are steered systematically into the better mousetraps and countless other goods and services uses that deliver the public most value. Every penny spent by consumers, in innumerable daily transactions, acts like a vote in a continual ballot. Each one sends out a signal to entrepreneurs, telling them exactly how much of each and every good and service should be produced. That prompts entrepreneurs to divert resources and production processes towards their most valued uses. It also prompts them to innovate and seek out new ways of creating and supplying better and better-value products. The result is that available resources are used as effectively as they can be. Value is enhanced and the whole society benefits.

> *"In the political democracy only the votes cast for the majority candidate or the majority plan are effective in shaping the course of affairs. The votes polled by the minority do not directly influence politics. But on the market no vote is cast in vain. Every penny spent has the power to work upon the production processes."*
>
> **—Ludwig von Mises, *Human Action***

Entrepreneurship and diversity

The mainstream economics approach has yet another shortcoming. It under-estimates, indeed ignores, the importance of diversity. In so-called 'perfect competition', products are identical. In reality, they are obviously not: think of the variety and choice we have in everyday goods: different kinds of tea, bread, footwear, hats, chairs, phones, cars or housing; and in different services too, like hairdressing, banking, entertainment, job training, transport or veterinary services. True, the 'perfect competition' model is only a theoretical abstraction that is designed to help us think. But by glossing over the real diversity and complexity of economic activity, it actually misleads us, and encourages some very mistaken ideas. It makes many people conclude, for example, that having more than one producer of anything—cars, chemicals, ships, paper, clothing or whatever else—must be 'wasteful'. After all, 'economies of scale' mean that a single large firm should be able to produce things far more cheaply than numerous small ones. At the same time, distribution systems could be unified and there would be no need for competitive advertising.

Yet, far from promoting any 'wasteful' duplication of identical products, real-life competition spurs entrepreneurs to create products that are *different*. They want to win customers from their competitors by offering them products that are not the same, but better or cheaper or both. They want to create products that stand out from the crowd, products that capture customers' attention and imagination, and make them switch their spending patterns. As a result, consumers enjoy a huge variety of products to choose from, with different features and at different levels of price and quality. No two models of car, computer or cosmetic are identical. Even seemingly standard products like soap or orange juice or hamburgers are made, styled, packaged and marketed in different ways. Nor would we even want to have the same clothes, footwear, watches or hairstyles as everyone else. Yet the 'perfect competition' model ignores this diversity and therefore overlooks the role and importance of entrepreneurship in creating it—and, indeed, in driving innovation and human progress.

In the real world, there is certainly plenty of competition. But entrepreneurs are *not* trying to give us all some identical product. They are striving to find out what sorts of products we *prefer.* That brings their ingenuity and innovation to bear on supplying what the public really wants. In the process, they make new discoveries, develop new systems, improve productivity, increase value and promote progress.

Those are all very important reasons why we should care about entrepreneurship and try to understand and encourage it.

3

Different views of entrepreneurship

Structures, roles, personalities

Most people imagine entrepreneurship in one of three ways: as a particular kind of business, as a specific occupation, or as a special kind of mindset that some people possess. It is worth exploring these common views in more detail.

Business type. Often, people equate entrepreneurship with start-up businesses. Some economists even use the number of new business start-ups as an index of how much entrepreneurship there is in a country. This is a mistake. First, as we have seen, a start-up business is not necessarily an entrepreneurial one. Large numbers of small cafes, tattoo parlours, cycle repair shops, dry cleaners and corner newsagents start up every year, but hardly any can really be called 'entrepreneurial'. Second, an entrepreneur does not necessarily have to start up a new business. It is true that many do prefer to create their own enterprises—through which they can pursue their ideas in their own way, develop their innovations without having to please bosses or shareholders, and reap the whole reward of their (hoped-for) success. But there can be entrepreneurship in older, established companies too. Ford, for instance, is developing car-sharing and parking-locator apps; Amazon is creating web services for other countries; IBM is thinking of artificial intelligence as a service rather than as hardware or software; Google is exploring self-driving cars, space research and other things. In fact, large businesses can be very effective at developing entrepreneurial innovations, having the resources to back them and the size to scale them up, even internationally.

Self-employment is not a good index of entrepreneurship either. Again, many people think of self-employed people as 'entrepreneurs' and imagine that entrepreneurs are all self-employed. But neither of those things is necessarily true. Self-employed plumbers or taxi-drivers are not usually described as 'entrepreneurs.' Neither are self-employed tour-guides, clowns, jewellery designers, personal trainers, journalists, cleaners, gardeners, pet-sitters or music teachers. The number of self-employed people is therefore not a good measure of entrepreneurship.

Indeed, it could be the very opposite: the *Global Entrepreneurship Monitor* suggests that entrepreneurial activity is *negatively* correlated with self-employment.[14] The reasons are numerous. For example, high levels of self-employment in a country might indicate that few people there have the incentive, drive, resources or opportunity to break out of working as sole traders and instead create their own successful, growing business. Or it may be that self-employed people in those places do not even start to think of growing their own enterprise because there is not enough capital around to make such an expansion feasible. Poor

....

14 *Global Entrepreneurship Monitor.* London: Global Entrepreneurship Research Association, London Business School.

infrastructure (e.g. communications and transport) may make it hard to scale up a business from the local area. Or perhaps there are such onerous regulations on employing other people that it is not worth the bother. Some of the poorest countries have high levels of self-employment; but that indicates only the prevalence of subsistence farming or home-based craft trades—not entrepreneurship. As if to underline that fact, statistics show that the more self-employed people a country has, the fewer billionaires it boasts.[15]

A lot of bad public policy stems from confusing entrepreneurship with start-ups or self-employment.[16] A slightly better indicator might be the number of *gazelles* (young, fast-growing enterprises with a large turnover and a record of revenue growth)[17] or even *unicorns* (privately held start-ups valued at over $1 billion—though as the name suggests, these are rare). Nevertheless, these measures focus only on the few successes that emerge from the entrepreneurial process. They massively understate the scale of entrepreneurship because they ignore the volume of entrepreneurial activity that occurs in established firms and also the vast bulk of personal entrepreneurial effort that ends in failure, as most do. Nor can these measures accurately compare the entrepreneurship rate between different countries or at different times. That is because different countries have different laws, taxes, regulations, institutions, infrastructure and capital markets. Such factors even change over time

15 Sanandaji, T. and Leeson, P. (2013) 'Billionaires'. In *Industrial and Corporate Change,* 22(1): 313–337.

16 Henrekson, M. and Sanandaji, T. (2008) 'Entrepreneurship and the Theory of Taxation.' *Research Institute of Industrial Economics*, IFN Working Paper No. 732.

17 Technically revenues of $1 million or more and revenue growth of 20% or more over four years.

within the same country. There may be plenty of entrepreneurs around in every age and every country, but the likelihood of them becoming gazelles or unicorns depends on many other things.

Occupation. Another way of defining an entrepreneur is as an owner-manager of a small company. The number of owner-managers can therefore be taken as a measure of how many entrepreneurs there are. That definition at least gives us the reassurance that some entrepreneurial mind is at work, organising and managing business resources. And it is true that most entrepreneurs are owner-managers or business partners.

But again, this definition seems too broad: we would not normally describe the owner-manager of a small café or a corner store, who never thinks of expanding it, as an entrepreneur. We are more likely to have in mind someone owning and managing a small business but trying to make it bigger and better by streamlining its production, developing new markets and managing growth. Moreover, not all entrepreneurs are owner-managers. Many may be employees of large companies; some may be creative people who leave the management of their business to others.

Some people define an entrepreneur as someone to whom creating, producing and marketing products is an occupation. They create one innovation after another. They might even start new businesses to pursue each one. These are what we call *serial* entrepreneurs. Examples abound: Steve Jobs (Apple, NeXT, Pixar), Elon Musk (SpaceX, Tesla, SolarCity), Sir Richard Branson (Virgin Music, Virgin Atlantic, Virgin Rail), and Sir James Dyson (vacuum cleaners, air purifiers, washing machines, hair dryers, lighting). But there are many others. One might even include Oprah Winfrey: known for her TV chat show in the US, she established Harpo Productions to exploit its rights, launched the Oprah Winfrey Network and is co-founder of the cable station

Oxygen. To many such serial entrepreneurs, already billionaires, the financial reward is no longer important; they simply seem driven to try new things.

Mindset. Is entrepreneurship then a mindset that separates out entrepreneurs from others? When speaking of entrepreneurs, most people think of their creativity, their inventiveness and search for novelty, their alertness to opportunities, their determination to disrupt the existing order, their personal identification with their business and its products, their single-minded commitment to style, quality and management. Alongside these characteristics might go confidence, experience, the ability to multitask and a willingness to take risks as crucial too.[18]

Not all entrepreneurs have all these personality traits, nor do they have them in equal measure. There are brilliant innovators and opportunity-spotters who are terrible managers, and inspiring managers who completely misinterpret the market. Silicon Valley abounds with 'nerds' and obsessives who cannot manage people, and highly competent managers who misunderstand their product and their market. Steve Jobs might be an example of the first, and John Sculley, who briefly ousted him from Apple, the second.

> *"I'm convinced that about half of what separates the successful entrepreneurs from the non-successful ones is pure perseverance."*
>
> **—Steve Jobs, Co-founder, Apple**

....

18 Foss, N. and P. Klein. (2010) 'Alertness, Action, and the Antecedents of Entrepreneurship.' In *The Journal of Private Enterprise* 25(2): 145-164.

Another problem is that these mindset traits are hard to measure. How can we put a number on 'alertness' or 'creativity' or 'determination'? As a way of knowing how much entrepreneurship we have, or whether public policy might be boosting or retarding it, they are not much help. Moreover, the mere fact that people have these traits is no indicator that they will succeed as entrepreneurs. They may have bold, imaginative and creative ideas but never get their enterprise out of start-up mode. Or they may grow their companies only to become complacent with their success and be overtaken by other bold, imaginative and creative people.[19] In a competitive economy, entrepreneurs need to stay sharp to stay on top.

Firm size and entrepreneurship

Large vs small. The Austrian political economist Joseph Schumpeter (1883-1950) originally thought that large firms would lead entrepreneurial innovation because they had the capital, the skilled and informed employees, and the marketing and distribution systems to make successes out of new products. But then when he was writing (1911), many of the current industrial technologies such as steel, textiles, electricity and oil required the economies of scale that only large businesses could provide.[20]

Later on, though, Schumpeter concluded that smaller companies could be more flexible and agile, and therefore possibly more entrepreneurial

19 See, for example, McMaken (2014).

20 Schumpeter, J. (1911) *The Theory of Economic Development*. New Brunswick and London: Transaction Publishers.

than large ones. The American economist William Baumol (1922-2017) agreed, arguing that the most radical and disruptive innovation came from start-up companies. Larger firms could also be entrepreneurial, but they tended to produce more incremental innovation.[21] There are several reasons why this might be. Large firms may be heavily invested in existing product lines, which might prompt them to focus on improving existing products and processes, rather than replacing them with something radically new. Being committed to their existing production technology, they might struggle to embrace new methods. Such issues can make life difficult for 'intrapreneurs' in large companies. Even so, many entrepreneurs get their start in larger businesses, where they learn about a particular industry, and perhaps see potential opportunities that they can exploit by starting up independently.

Complex factors. However, the picture is more complicated than this. Most start-ups will fail. Only one in 17,000 American companies grow to be worth $500 million, according to the international consultants Bain & Co.[22] By contrast, established firms that leverage their core business have about a 1-in-8 change of creating a viable large-scale new business. That makes the chances of success in a large firm about 2,000 times higher than in a start-up.

....

21 Baumol, W. (2002) *The Free-Market Innovation Machine: Analyzing the Growth Miracle of Capitalism*. Princeton University Press.

22 Zook, C. and Allen, J. (2016) *Barriers and Pathways to Sustainable Growth: Harnessing the Power of the Founder's Mentality. Bain & Co.*, July 19.

> *"The life of a start-up is full of ups and downs, an emotional roller coaster ride that you can't quite imagine if you've spent your whole career in a corporation."*
>
> **—Harvey Mackay, US businessman and columnist**

As Schumpeter realised, salaried employees of large firms can be entrepreneurs too.[23] But large firms need to have a strategy in place for supporting them. From their daily activities, corporate intrapreneurs may be keenly aware of the needs of customers, and they may have the tenacity to find and develop new products; but they still need to get their firm to support their ideas. Large firms have to be 'ambidextrous'.[24] They have to connect their processes, in manufacture and marketing, to innovation. That means aligning structures and projects and personnel. It means creating a culture that welcomes a multiplicity of ideas and experiments—not always easy, given the inertia that is often associated with size.

Large-small partnerships. Mindful of this, many large firms develop partnerships with smaller entrepreneurial operations. Some organise innovation competitions for start-ups or students who are about to

....

23 Schumpeter, J. (1939) *Business Cycles: A Theoretical, Historical and Statistical Analysis of the Capitalist Process.* New York: McGraw-Hill.

24 March, J. (1991) 'Whither Exploration and Exploitation.' *Organization Science* 2(1): 71-87.

graduate. That helps them to identify future technologies and draw innovators into their sphere. Innovations like the cloud and big data, for example, have endless possible applications, so it is valuable to have large numbers of fresh minds working on such issues, rather than commit to some single corporate approach.

Nevertheless, trying to identify future innovators to invest in is a gamble. Less riskily, large firms might instead search for firms that are closer to bringing products to market, and which might enhance or complement their own business.

Some large firms act as 'accelerators', speeding the growth of smaller entrepreneurial companies by providing advice and capital. That allows them to upgrade their own processes or product offerings in exchange for advice, investment, a ready marketing system and often a better understanding of customer interests than many innovators might have themselves.

Other large firms support 'incubators' that gestate disruptive ideas in the hope of creating something completely new that complements or updates their existing offerings. PSA Peugeot-Citroën, for instance, sees its future in providing 'mobility solutions' rather than just building cars, and is encouraging the development of new ideas to this end. IBM too sees its future as a provider of services to business, rather than a maker of machines. Such partnerships allow large firms to filter new developments and make use of a much wider spectrum of ideas, all at less cost and risk than they might be able to do themselves.

Kinds of entrepreneur

Individuals and groups. Entrepreneurs, then, are not always owner-managers who work alone. As we have seen, they might be 'intrapreneurs' employed by large companies; but they might also be innovators in small and growing businesses who collaborate with larger firms for mutual benefit.

Nor do independent entrepreneurs always work alone. Many establish themselves in partnerships, such as Larry Page and Sergey Brin of Google, Steve Jobs and Steve Wozniak at Apple, Bill Hewlett and Dave Packard from Hewlett-Packard, Ben Cohen and Jerry Greenfield of Ben & Jerry's, William Procter and James Gamble of Procter & Gamble. The advantage of this is that the partners may have different, but complementary skills, to cover each other's deficiencies, and provide a critical friend on whom to test ideas. In other cases, larger groups of individuals come together to found and grow companies. Even companies themselves can form new entrepreneurial partnerships—for example Apple's partnering with MasterCard to create a new entrepreneurial concept, ApplePay.

Innovators and managers. To succeed, entrepreneurs need to be able to do more than have innovative ideas or keep alert to market opportunities. They actually have to turn their vision into reality. That means not only initiating an enterprise but steering it through to fruition, which entails a good deal of management effort as well. At the very least, that requires them to draw together resources such as personnel and capital, and to focus those resources on delivering their vision.

They might well hire in others for their management skills and leave them to handle the details—such as registering a company, obtaining licences, complying with regulations, researching markets or negotiating with capital providers, landlords and staff. But they still have to direct those managers, manage their own investments, combine resources and understand the market they are trying to engage with. In that sense, entrepreneurs have to be managers too.

Non-commercial entrepreneurs. Economists naturally tend to think of entrepreneurs and entrepreneurship in a business, trade or commercial setting. Indeed, some argue that the pursuit of financial profit is a key part of the definition of entrepreneurship.

In common language, however, we speak of entrepreneurship as something found in non-commercial settings too. We talk of 'social entrepreneurs' who search for solutions to social, cultural or environmental problems, not necessarily for self-gain. They may devise ways to alleviate poverty by organising and providing food banks, say, or invent new forms of low-cost housing, or find better means of giving people access to healthcare and education. They may develop new systems to raise money for good causes, or to help philanthropists direct their donations more effectively. There are even 'academic entrepreneurs' who create new fields of research, and 'policy entrepreneurs' who inject ideas into the public debate, serving the general interest rather than their own.

Nor does common language limit entrepreneurship to philanthropic activities. We can even speak of people who work out clever schemes to get around regulations or tax laws as being 'entrepreneurial'—though we may not admire them for it. Nevertheless, in the everyday way of speaking, it is clear that 'entrepreneurship' in its most general sense is all around us.

Entrepreneurs are unusual people

To most economists, however, entrepreneurship is a much rarer thing. Its rarity is inevitable, given what commercial entrepreneurs have to deal with. They face complex choices of what to produce and how to produce it. Not everyone has the necessary qualities to succeed at this.

Entrepreneurial orientation. The idea of entrepreneurship implies a departure from existing products and existing ways of doing things. It requires not only innovation but the marshalling of resources too. Since entrepreneurs are not simply following the market, they cannot simply copy what others do in this regard, but have to invent new structures of their own. Inevitably they take risks, on whether their structures will work and whether their product will prove attractive to future customers. Economists call this combination of innovativeness, proactiveness and risk-taking as *entrepreneurial orientation*.[25] Entrepreneurs need all three qualities. A firm that takes risks by borrowing heavily but produces nothing new is not normally thought of as 'entrepreneurial'. Nor is a firm that merely copies others rather than consciously creating some innovative product or technology.

The entrepreneurial process. With these points in mind, some economists see entrepreneurship as a *process*—involving not just complex choices, but a long string of complex choices that must be got right if the entrepreneur is to succeed. It starts with *being aware* and then *spotting opportunities* (arising from technological, social, regulatory, or market changes, for example); then *forming a view* on whether or not

....

25 Miller, D. (1983) 'The Correlates of Entrepreneurship in Three Types of Firms'. *Management Science* 29(7).

those opportunities might be worth grasping; *making guesses* about the future state of the market and of customer demand; calmly *assessing the risks* and *evaluating* whether the costs of seizing the opportunity might be worth the costs (e.g. the time, mental and physical effort and money) of doing so. It then involves *developing* the best products and processes to use; *identifying, acquiring and assembling* the necessary resources; *creating and launching* a new venture; *focusing* those resources on delivering that vision; *product design*; and *marketing*. An independent entrepreneur must then achieve *early success* and *build* on it; *scale up* the enterprise and *manage growth.* Every entrepreneurial firm must *respond to changes* in outcomes, markets, supply and demand conditions, taxes, regulations and institutions; *check* at each stage that resources are and remain well invested and well organised; and more. This is no quick and easy operation and the skills to master all its stages are not common.

That may be why only 1-2% of people in the workforce start a new business in any one year—and why most fail. Yet the few who succeed as entrepreneurs are vital to us all. They raise the competitiveness and productivity of the whole economy. They boost growth by developing new technologies, and better, cheaper products. They challenge existing suppliers to shape up or leave the market. With more productive new firms coming in and less productive ones dropping out, the overall mix of firms is made more productive and better suited to market realities. And this rising productivity and focus promotes rising prosperity for everyone.

The entrepreneurial mind

What is it, then, that drives people to risk their time, effort and money for uncertain results in the long and complex process of entrepreneurship? The glib answer is the lure of financial profit. But that is not always so. Some 'lifestyle' entrepreneurs simply want to be their own boss and love the freedom of independence that this brings. Others simply love the thrill of starting new enterprises and seeing their hunches proved right.

Personality. Entrepreneurial minds seem to focus more on opportunity than risk. In fact, entrepreneurs and potential entrepreneurs may be *over*-optimistic: the *Global Entrepreneurship Monitor* reports that two-fifths (40%) of Americans think it is easy to start a business, and nearly half (49%) think they could run one.[26] Given the high failure rate of new businesses, they are plainly mistaken on both counts.

Creativity is important, but successful entrepreneurs also tend to have a strong work ethic, drive and ambition. Many have great self-confidence, energy and strong leadership abilities. They tend to be adaptive, resilient, and able to deal with failure and with stress. According to the American economist Deirdre McCloskey (1977-), they also require good social skills such as the ability to persuade and inspire trust in others such as suppliers, investors, co-workers and customers.[27]

Inheritance. Most entrepreneurs are self-made. Even in the UK, where—more than most places—social class and inheritance are commonly regarded as the main source of wealth, the annual *Rich List* published by the *Sunday Times* newspaper reveals that around

....

26 Bosma, Niels and Donna Kelley (2019) '2018/2019 Global Report.' *Global Entrepreneurship Monitor*

27 McCloskey, D. (1994) *Knowledge and Persuasion in Economics*. New York: Cambridge University Press. See also McCloskey D. and Klamer A. (1995) 'One Quarter of GDP is Persuasion.' *American Economic Review*, Papers and Proceedings 85(2): 191–95.

95% of the richest 1000 UK entrepreneurs are actually self-made. Worldwide, the annual *Billionaire Census* compiled by the market research firm Wealth-X suggests that fewer than one in seven (13%) of world billionaires inherited their wealth, while well over half (56%) are completely self-made. Many of the rest have inherited a small family business but changed it out of all recognition.[28] The annual *Forbes* billionaire list reports broadly similar figures.

Financial profit. The desire for financial profit might be a factor that weighs more heavily in the theories of economists than in the minds of entrepreneurs. Most entrepreneurs report that the main consideration for them is not money, but that they love what they do. To many, profit may be little more than a mark of personal success or social standing. Many super-entrepreneurs cannot possibly spend all the money they earn but are still enthusiastically active in creating new products and developing new initiatives. To them, it is more like a game than a financial pursuit, and it is the thrill of the game and the satisfaction of success that is their reward.

Education. Entrepreneurial success is also based on knowledge and understanding—of technologies, markets, institutions and people. Creativity, innovation and management all demand intellectual facility, grounded in facts and experience. Education, therefore, can be a positive factor in promoting entrepreneurship and helping entrepreneurs succeed.

The statistics show that super-entrepreneurs are well educated, with

28 Wealth-X (2019). 'The Wealth-X Billionaire Census 2019.'

more higher degrees than the average; in the US they have five times more PhDs than the rest of the population, though that may reflect the nature of the knowledge-based tech industries that have sprung up in Silicon Valley and other parts of that country. Only a third (33%) of American small business owners have no higher education at all.[29]

Experience. Nevertheless, experience may count for more than formal education. Less than a tenth (9%) of US small business owners have a business degree. And many super-entrepreneurs dropped out of college (e.g. Facebook's Mark Zuckerberg, fashion designer Ralph Lauren, computer entrepreneur Michael Dell, Microsoft founder Bill Gates, Apple cofounder Steve Jobs and Uber co-founder Travis Kalanick). Indeed, one in eight *Forbes*-listed billionaires dropped out. Others never went to college at all (e.g. inventor Sir Clive Sinclair, designer Coco Chanel, serial entrepreneur Sir Richard Branson and IKEA founder Ingvar Kampgrad).

There may be good reasons for this. Some super-entrepreneurs learn just enough at college to give them good ideas that can be turned into profit. But people who actually graduate from college tend to be more risk averse than others. Academic ability is not the same as having ideas and being able to run a company and may well be inimical to it: academics do not usually turn into entrepreneurs (though there are some). By contrast, most successful entrepreneurs are people with a good deal of life experience; in the US, well over half (60%) are over 40, and a substantial number have gone through personal difficulties such as failed businesses or divorce. (Indeed, at least one UK venture

29 Sanandaji, T. and Sanandaji, N. (2014).

capitalist believes that divorce—though no more than one divorce—is a good measure of whether a business founder is likely to succeed commercially.)

Sociological factors

Many analysts have argued that sociological factors including culture, religion and demography may promote entrepreneurship. For example, a society that places high value on self-help, hard work, aspiration and courage may produce more entrepreneurs than others. Likewise, a society that honours champions or motivates people to succeed might stimulate, in potential entrepreneurs, the desire to be the best at what they do. And a society that is not afraid of change, and sees opportunities in it rather than threats, may again promote (or at least not resist) the sort of radical changes that entrepreneurs produce.

Values. Shared moral principles such as honesty, a sense of justice and the respect for people's property rights might well promote entrepreneurship. Family values too may help: a strong family provides the succour that an entrepreneur might need to run a risky business—not to mention family members to 'mind the shop' when necessary. Religious values, too, might be significant. The German sociologist Max Weber (1864-1920) believed that the Protestant countries of Northern Europe were more successful economically because they put greater religious value on worldly action: while the next world was undoubtedly important, their theology maintained that working to use this world's resources in beneficial ways helped others and was virtuous too.[30]

....

30 Weber, M. (1905) *The Protestant Ethic and the Spirit of Capitalism.*

Migration. Minority groups often make good entrepreneurs. In the UK, for example, one seventh (14%) of start-up entrepreneurs are foreign-born, and nearly half (49%) of fast-growing new businesses have at least one foreign-born co-founder.[31] In the US, similarly, a high proportion of entrepreneurs are immigrants. Indeed, one study from 2016 found that immigrants founded over half of America's start-up companies that had grown to be valued at $1 billion or more.[32]

Various explanations for this have been put forward. Some observers have argued that minority groups have a need to prove themselves, which stimulates them to succeed. Others suggest that it is the 'cultural frontier'—that immigrants come with different ideas and can spot opportunities that the locals, through long familiarity, may miss.

31 Dumitriu, S. and Stewart, A. (2019) 'Job Creators: the Immigrant Founders of Britain's Fastest Growing Companies.' *The Entrepreneurs Network*.

32 Anderson, S. (2016) 'Immigrants and Billion Dollar Startups.' *National Foundation for American Policy*, Policy Brief, March.

4

The economic role of entrepreneurship

Thus far we have looked at entrepreneurship in terms of the common way that ordinary people think about it. Economists, however, see entrepreneurship in a different way and have their own views about what the *economic* role of entrepreneurship actually is. At least, those who think about the subject at all do.

Economics and uncertainty

The mainstream economic textbooks, as already mentioned, have relatively little to say on the subject of entrepreneurship. The core reason for this is perhaps that economists, envying the success of the natural sciences, have tended to model their own subject on the natural sciences like physics and mechanics. As a result, they picture economic activity as an interplay of impersonal forces; they attempt to explain, quantify and predict the results using numerical measures, correlations, graphs and formulae.

In reality, economic life is nothing like that. Even expert investors cannot accurately forecast daily stock prices or weekly exchange rates. Nor can central banks, with all the resources available to them, accurately predict the next quarter's economic growth. Such things are impossible because economic life is not an impersonal mechanism. It is the complex result of the unknowable personal aims and the countless different actions of diverse individuals who each face different and changing circumstances. It is also affected by natural and other events that we cannot anticipate with any confidence—tsunamis and droughts, for example, or discoveries and lucky accidents.

Since markets are in constant flux, and since we do not fully understand what moves them, those who are active in the market, such as entrepreneurs, can do no more than act on their best guesses. As the Chicago economist Frank Knight (1885-1972) put it, market players have to navigate both risk and uncertainty.[33] *Risk* is where we can quantify the *probability* of certain events (e.g. a casino operator can calculate mathematically the long-run odds of making a profit on a roulette wheel and even, through experience, the same on the blackjack tables). *Uncertainty* is where we have no information on which to make predictions (e.g. that changes in political events or moral attitudes will conspire to force casinos out of business entirely). Entrepreneurs have to make their best guesses about the future. And they may well come to different opinions as to what will succeed.

With this in mind, some economists see entrepreneurs primarily as people who *direct resources* in the face of *risk and uncertainty*. Others stress that entrepreneurs are individuals who are responsible for pursuing the *risks and benefits* of pursuing their particular vision of the future. Some have emphasised the *disruptive* nature of entrepreneurs as they introduce innovations that challenge the existing order. Others,

33 Knight, F. (1921) *Risk, Uncertainty and Profit.* Boston and New York: Houghton Mifflin Company.

by contrast, see entrepreneurs as people who are *alert to opportunities* and who fill gaps, *restoring* order in markets. It is worth looking at some of these different interpretations, starting again with the textbook approach.

The textbook model

The mainstream ideas of 'perfect competition' and 'equilibrium' (where markets settle into perfect balance), assume away innovation and change. In these mechanical models there is no human motivation, no need for new products or processes, no explanation of why new firms are created or fail, and therefore no purpose for entrepreneurship. Every fleeting disruption in supply or demand repairs itself, and everything returns swiftly and automatically into balance.

But as the Austro-American economist Ludwig von Mises (1881-1973) pointed out, there is no reason to believe any of that at all.[34] Human beings make mistakes and act on predictions that turn out to be false. As a result, markets are never going to be perfect and self-correcting. Moreover, it takes time and—entrepreneurial—action to plug gaps, repair mismatches and correct imbalances. Even before that has happened, things will have moved on again, and yet further gaps and mismatches will have opened up.

If markets were perfect, there would be no role for entrepreneurs (or anyone) to do anything at all. Since nobody can improve on perfection, why bother? The very fact that markets are not perfect is what motivates people to action. They take action in the hope of improving life. Entrepreneurs do this in various ways: spotting mismatches in supply and demand; creating new and better technologies and products; and taking

....

34 Mises, L. (1951) 'Profit and Loss.' In *Planning for Freedom*. South Holland, Ill.: Libertarian Press.

risks and organising resources to that end. That requires them to actively and mindfully mix labour and capital, manage production and market their products, according to their best judgement about an uncertain future.

Furthermore, the inputs they must put together are complex. No two parcels of land are identical, no two workers have identical skills, no two pieces of capital equipment are necessarily interchangeable. That diversity is ignored by the textbooks —which talk about the 'stock' of labour and capital as if all plumbers, farmers and ballerinas, or all trucks, printing presses and computers were the same. The fact that they are not makes combining resources both complex and risky. Additionally, entrepreneurs must invest their own time, energy and 'human capital' skills. And they need to convince others to trust them and join with them.

Most will not anticipate the future correctly or will struggle to manage resources or will fail to enjoin others, and their business will fail. But those failures still provide a useful lesson to them and to others, while their few successes promote the general prosperity of the whole population. That is because, in an open and competitive economy, the only source of financial profit is customers who voluntarily part with money in exchange for something they value more—the entrepreneur's product. After all, neither would bother to exchange unless they both considered themselves better off by it. The wider free exchange is, the more value is created and spread throughout the community—something the Scottish economist Adam Smith (1723-1790) noted 250 years ago.[35]

....

35 Smith, A. (1776) *An Inquiry into the Nature and Causes of the Wealth of Nations*.

"You don't learn to walk by following rules. You learn by doing and falling over."

—Sir Richard Branson, founder, Virgin Group

The entrepreneur as creative disruptor

The idea of the entrepreneur as an *innovator* and *disruptor* is associated principally with Joseph Schumpeter. To him, the key role of the entrepreneur was innovation. That did not mean merely inventing or discovering new things but also having new *business ideas* and forming innovative *growth-focused firms*. That process might involve using new combinations of resources to create new and better technologies or products. Or discovering and acting on new information that makes new products possible. Or opening up new markets or new sources of supply. Each implies the entrepreneur abandoning the common way of thinking and creating something new and different. It implies having a dream and the abilities to make it happen.

With all this in mind, Schumpeter regarded entrepreneurship and entrepreneurial innovation as a disruptive force. Constant innovation brought constant disruption but it was still vital for economic advance. It not only expanded the range and quality of products available to customers, it also inspired new production methods and created whole new industries, even clusters of industries. And those new methods and products themselves became resources that future entrepreneurs can use to create yet other products—as the microchip became for the producers of computers, and computers became for the development of driverless cars.

> *"The essential point to grasp is that in dealing with capitalism we are dealing with an evolutionary process."*
>
> **—Joseph A Schumpeter, *Capitalism, Socialism and Democracy***

Creative disruption. As pioneers were copied by others, thought Schumpeter, new methods and products would spread. Unable to compete, old industries would decline, and old jobs might be lost. But that too has a benefit: it leaves labour and other resources available to be re-focused on the creation of higher-value products and processes. Schumpeter called this process 'creative destruction'.

The phrase is unfortunate, because it focuses attention on the 'destruction' and suggests that capitalism and entrepreneurship are a threat to jobs. Perhaps 'creative disruption' might have been a happier term. But Schumpeter wanted to emphasise the dynamism of entrepreneurial innovation, shifting resources to more productive uses, in contrast to the textbook notion that markets naturally remained stable and balanced.

While entrepreneurial change is disruptive, it is rarely destructive, except in radical circumstances where completely new technologies suddenly make entire old industries redundant—e.g. online maps replacing printed atlases, digital photography replacing film, or word processors replacing typewriters. In most cases, the transition is less rapid, and producers have more time to adjust. For example, motor vehicles replaced horse-drawn ones only slowly, because they remained expensive luxuries—at least, until another innovation, Henry Ford's mass production process, made them cheaper. Certainly, the industrial landscape of many countries is disfigured by the hulks of abandoned mines, factories and docks, all testament to the 'destruction' inherent in Schumpeter's 'creative destruction'. Yet the obvious creative benefits of economic advance must be set against those losses. None of us would want to give up the many innovations that gave us wealth and leisure, to go back to spending our whole waking lives finding and carrying back food, water and fuel.

The entrepreneur as discoverer

Another—arguably incompatible—view of the economic role of the entrepreneur comes from the prominent Anglo-American economist Israel Kirzner (1930-). To Kirzner, entrepreneurship means *being alert* to untapped profit opportunities and attempting to realise those profits. Entrepreneurs, being alert, notice gaps and mismatches that others have not yet seen—unsatisfied demand, say, or prices that do not fully reflect market conditions—and move to profit by acting on those discoveries.[36]

> *"Entrepreneurs see change as the norm and as healthy. Usually, they do not bring about the change themselves. But—and this defines entrepreneur and entrepreneurship—the entrepreneur always searches for change, responds to it, and exploits it as an opportunity."*
>
> **– Peter F. Drucker, *Innovation and Entrepreneurship***

....

36 Kirzner, I. (1973) *Competition and Entrepreneurship*. Chicago and London: University of Chicago Press.

This kind of entrepreneurship seems more commonplace than Schumpeter's creative disruptors. It does not rely on a few people with innovative genius. Indeed, all of us look for opportunities—hunting for better jobs, for example, or taking a training course to make ourselves more employable. We do not even have to be very alert: sometimes we are just the right person in the right place to take advantage of what turns up: we merely have to grasp the opportunity. And, of course, to decide to see it through. Kirzner's entrepreneur is primarily an opportunity-spotter but also a decision-maker.

Entrepreneurs and coordination. Instead of disrupting markets, this entrepreneur is someone who restores order to them. Markets generally work well, but they are never perfect, and mistakes do occur. There may be gaps in people's knowledge about the potential of new technologies, say, or confusion about the true state of supply and demand conditions, causing things to go out of sync. Kirzner's entrepreneur sees such gaps and mismatches not as problems but as profit opportunities. And in pursuing that profit, the entrepreneur actually helps to close the gaps. For example, entrepreneurs might notice that market prices are out of step with the real state of supply or demand and then start buying things they believe are under-priced or selling things that they believe are overpriced—much as stockbrokers and asset managers do every day. Their motive is to make a financial profit, but their action also has the effect of bidding up the price of the under-valued items and bidding down the price of the over-expensive ones. That prompts prices to come back into balance—all the more so when others see what they are doing and copy it.

Kirzner therefore sees the entrepreneur as someone who promotes the coordination of economic resources, rather than someone who disrupts things. If markets are out of kilter, he maintains, it is because market players are ignorant of something and do not spot the opportunity to correct the mistake. However, the alertness and action of entrepreneurs helps spread a greater awareness of the real facts. As they and their imitators drive prices up or down, resources are drawn into more-valued uses and away from less-valued ones.

Entrepreneurs as information processors

That is not to say that buying low and selling high is easy. Entrepreneurs cannot know everything about the present, and the future is even more uncertain. In addition, products take time to design, manufacture and bring to market; so, entrepreneurs must try to anticipate and fill *future* gaps in supply and demand. Since nobody can predict the future for sure, entrepreneurs need to *take a view* on how things might turn out. There is no 'right' view: different entrepreneurs will take different positions, based on their different appetites for risk and their assessments of future uncertainties.

Certainly, they are more likely to succeed if their view is *informed.* So, they may invest in research and testing to understand what potential customers might choose, to establish what production options exist and to explore the viability of their business idea. But they will still have to make decisions on information that is uncertain, incomplete, scattered and often hard to obtain and interpret.

"What makes profit emerge is the fact that the entrepreneur who judges the future prices of the products more correctly than other people do buy some or all of the factors of production at prices which, seen from the point of view of the future state of the market, are too low."

—Ludwig von Mises, *Profit and Loss*

Entrepreneurs must also consider the countless other uses of their time, energy and capital—what economists call *opportunity costs*—and to assess which of many possible strategies might be the most fruitful. Yet as the German economist Ludwig Lachmann (1906-1990) noted, there is a multiplicity of human purposes, a multiplicity of possible goods that *could* be produced to satisfy them, and a multiplicity of different ways of producing those goods.[37] Choosing between them is no straightforward task.

Given the multiplicity of choices, entrepreneurs have to experiment not just with new products but with new production technologies and processes. They combine different inputs, evaluate the results and then try other combinations in order to make their productive networks as productive and cost-effective as they can in producing what their customers actually want. Again, there are many possibilities to juggle with, and it is not surprising that many mistakes are made. But with many entrepreneurs all experimenting competitively with different

37 Lachmann, L. (1986) *The Market as an Economic Process.* New York: Basil Blackwell.

products and processes, knowledge is gained and spread. The long-run productivity of the whole economy is raised—which benefits everyone.

> *"We are living in a world of unexpected change; hence capital combinations ... will be ever changing, will be dissolved and reformed. In this activity, we find the real function of the entrepreneur."*
>
> **—Ludwig Lachmann, *The Market as an Economic Process***

Entrepreneurs and uncertainty

This is a continuous process. Entrepreneurs can never create a 'perfect' product, nor a 'perfect' production method. It is always possible that another will top them. The most we can say is that in competitive markets, *less successful* products and processes give way to *more successful* ones.[38] They do not have to be perfect and forever—merely better fitted to the market conditions that happen to prevail at the time. But inevitably, those conditions too will change. The supply of oil or foodstuffs might be hit by wars or droughts, for instance, or the demand for disability scooters might rise because the population is getting older and richer. Such changes will open up opportunities for yet other entrepreneurs to come along and fill the gaps.

Since markets are never at rest, entrepreneurs must make their production choices within a very risky and uncertain environment.

38 Mises, L. (1951) *Profit and Loss*. South Holland, Illinois: Consumer-Producers Economic Service.

But Kirzner (say his critics) overlooks this risk and uncertainty. His entrepreneur is on the alert for gaps to fill: but spotting gaps is the easy part. The real problem is that it takes time to design, produce and market a solution that coordinates things again. By then other changes may have occurred and the entrepreneur's guess is out of date before it is born.

Entrepreneurs and judgement

Building on this, the American economist Peter G Klein (1966-) suggests that the defining characteristic of entrepreneurship is *judgement under uncertainty*. The entrepreneur faces an uncertain future and must *take a view* about how things might turn out. Nobody can know that outcome for sure, of course: hence the need for judgement. Research and experience may help the entrepreneur, but as Mises put it, entrepreneurial judgement "defies any rules and systematisation. It can be neither taught nor learned."[39] Entrepreneurs must make plans, focus resources and produce the products they hope will succeed on the basis of *their own particular view* of how future market conditions will turn out.

It is the diversity of those views that makes entrepreneurship potentially profitable. If everyone thought that nuclear fusion was on the verge of bringing the world safe and virtually free energy, they would all scramble to invest in it and the potential profits would be spread very thinly between them. Significant profits come to entrepreneurs only when they make correct judgements while others are making wrong ones. As Mises again put it, an entrepreneur sees the future differently from others. That is why entrepreneurs are able to buy and assemble

....

39 Mises, L. (1949) Chapter 9 in *Human Action*. Yale University Press.

low-cost resources today in order to produce high-price services in the future, without everyone else bidding up their costs.

The former head of IBM, Thomas Watson, probably never uttered his supposed 1943 statement, "I think there is a world market for maybe five computers." But that was not an uncommon view in the 1940s and 1950s. Then, computers took up whole floors and were so expensive that only the largest institutions could afford one. Their potential was regarded as largely limited to solving specialist mathematical problems. As the technology advanced, however, others such as Steve Jobs of Apple took a radically different view—that everyone would demand affordable, user-friendly home computers to help with a wide variety of everyday tasks. He also had the creativity and drive to make that happen. As IBM lost its market dominance, Jobs made a fortune out of his vision and judgement. It is hard to find a better example of what we all understand by an 'entrepreneur'.

5

The importance of entrepreneurship

Some of the economic benefits of entrepreneurship (such as raising productivity and steering resources to higher value uses) have already been mentioned. But there are other benefits, both economic and social, which it generates too.

Economic benefits

Product improvement. As we have seen, entrepreneurship spurs economic *growth* by enabling us to produce *more*. But it also spurs economic *development* by enabling us to produce *better*. Entrepreneurs look for new and better production technologies to raise productivity and create products that are not just cheaper and more plentiful but more useful and higher quality too.

The results are evident. Our cars break down less often. They also warn us of problems, are more fuel-efficient and park themselves. Our computers are smaller, faster and better networked. Our suitcases are lighter and stronger and have polyurethane wheels that save us struggling to carry them. We no longer get our fingers stained because our pens do not need to be filled each day from a bottle of ink. Bulky gramophones have given way to tiny pocket devices that give us instant access to the best performances of the world's best musicians at a superb level of quality. Our televisions are larger, slimmer, sharper and smarter. Our toothbrushes are electric and tell us if we are brushing properly or not. Our books take up no space at all on our pocket readers. Shampoo no longer stings our eyes. Soon our cars will drive themselves, and all these other products will be improved on too.

Entrepreneurs provide customers with products that improve their lives, sometimes dramatically, as (say) an industrial robot can do for a manufacturer, bubble wrap can do for a retailer, a hearing aid can do for a deaf person or a smartphone can do for just about anyone. And this progress continues on.

Better information. Entrepreneurs' activities also spread information about which processes are better and which products are most valued. By experimenting with new ways of combining and using inputs to cost and improving product quality, they reveal better ways of working to others. By buying up resources that they think are undervalued, or selling things they consider overvalued, they alert others to those opportunities. By supplying products that customers actively prefer, they show others where the demand is.

The spread of better and more complete information in this way improves the operation and efficiency of markets. As others strive to copy the pioneering entrepreneurs' success, they draw resources such as capital and labour from less valued applications and direct them to the more valued ones, helping to generate more value out of fewer resources.

Cascading development. Sometimes, entrepreneurs' products enable the development of other products or even whole industries. For example, microprocessors and touchscreens made possible tablets and smartphones, which in turn made possible ride-sharing apps and paperless ticketing.

The rise of the IT and communications industries in India during the 1990s unleashed a similar sort of cascade, making possible new businesses such as call centres, and creating demand for new construction, networks, hardware, software and maintenance, all of which boosted employment. Greater connectivity, nationally and internationally, made people more aware of market conditions outside their own community, allowing a new generation of entrepreneurs to see and exploit opportunities not just locally but globally.

Nor was this development merely economic. The new employment opportunities in India drew people away from a harsh agricultural existence and into a more prosperous and comfortable life in the cities. Education and training bodies arose, or expanded, to teach skills to the new workers. The new industries also started to break down the caste system, since they needed employees with skill and brains, regardless of their caste. Meanwhile, even those who remained on the land benefited from the IT revolution. Women created new businesses renting out mobile phones to others in their villages. And with web-enabled phones, farmers now could check the prices of their rice, wheat, cotton, sugarcane, onions or tea in commodities markets hundreds of miles away, and negotiate better prices for themselves instead of having to accept what local agents might offer.

Rising productivity

Long-term improvement. As new and more productive firms spring up, creating cheaper and better products and getting them to customers more effectively, older and less productive businesses lose market share. They may even drop out entirely. But in turn the new firms may be supplanted by yet other enterprises that produce even better products even more efficiently. The result is a systematic and long-term improvement in economic productivity and value creation. Resources such as labour and capital are drawn into more highly valued uses, more and better products are produced using fewer and cheaper inputs.

Internationalism. Indeed, this happens on an international scale. Financial capital is highly mobile. No longer do entrepreneurs have to save up their own money to expand their business, or rely on money from friends, family or local investors. If their idea is promising and they have good management skills and a strong business case, they can tap capital markets anywhere in the world, borrowing the funds they need or selling a share in their business in return for capital. That is particularly important for entrepreneurs in poorer countries, where local funding is hard to find. Potentially it gives them access to the same funding that is available to entrepreneurs in even the richest countries.

The same internationalism applies to management as well. Like financial capital, 'human capital' is mobile; managers and consultants can take their skills to any country where they are appreciated. Again, this is particularly valuable to entrepreneurs in poorer countries where management education and training may be less advanced and where good managers may be hard to find. Like access to capital, access to better management and advice helps entrepreneurs to boost their productivity, and with it, the productivity and prosperity of their community and country.

Research and development. There are other economic benefits too. Being focused on improving products and processes, entrepreneurs are commonly a focus of research and development, creating new understandings, new ventures, new technologies and new products, as well as researching and opening up new markets. Established industries may hit a revenue ceiling as the demand for their product becomes fully satisfied. But new products open up the untapped market demand for something better or cheaper. As better products become more plentiful and more affordable, the public experiences a rise in wealth; while the new production processes generate new employment opportunities and the prospect of higher earnings. Indeed, most new jobs come from small businesses and start-ups.

Human benefits

There are human and social benefits from entrepreneurship as well as the economic ones. Entrepreneurs' focus on delivering new and better products make us less dependent on old, slow and often labour-intensive technologies. Our grandparents would spend hours each day bringing buckets of coal into the house, making up the fire, cleaning out the ash and disposing of it afterwards. Modern central heating takes up no time at all. Our grandparents also spent days each week washing clothes on a scrubbing board, putting them through a mangle, drying them on a line (weather permitting) and then pressing them with irons that were heated on the fire. Now we have automatic washer/dryers and non-iron fabrics. Nor do these improvements reflect some inevitable march of technology: they exist only because entrepreneurs have purposefully created them.

The result of these and many other improvements, in sectors from agriculture through healthcare and retail to transport and more, is that we have a galaxy of diverse products to choose from. We do not have to spend so much time worrying about basic necessities and comforts. Entrepreneurial innovations make our work more productive—and also easier, with less manual labour and risk of injury—and our leisure more plentiful and rewarding, with more time to ourselves.

Furthermore, new entrepreneurial firms open up employment opportunities. That is particularly beneficial for migrants, minorities, young people and women who may be discriminated against by the workers and managers in larger, established industries. It allows workers to build up the savings and capital they need to improve their lives and undertake the education that will further boost their 'human capital' and employability. These are all personal and human benefits, not just dry 'economic' ones.

Social benefits

There are social benefits too. A community that has a diversity of entrepreneurial businesses is likely to be much more stable and relaxed than one which is dominated by some large heavy industry—a large mine, steel works or carmaker for example. Change and development can then happen gradually. Businesses can come and go, and workers can move between them as they choose. They do not live in fear of massive widespread unemployment should the dominant employer collapse.

Also, successful entrepreneurs are large investors in charities and community projects. There may of course be a strictly business motive behind that. Perhaps they may hope to promote goodwill towards the business among suppliers, workers and customers. By supporting local schools and hospitals, they may be able to recruit a healthier and more skilled workforce. By improving the local environment, they may improve their workers' morale and retain them for longer. They may even promote higher education, research and development projects in the hope of them discovering new opportunities that their business could potentially exploit.

Yet much of entrepreneurs' charitable activity is purely philanthropic. The Scottish-American steel magnate Andrew Carnegie (1835-1919) spent much of his fortune establishing and improving free public libraries. Through the Bill & Melinda Gates Foundation, the Microsoft entrepreneur directs thousands of millions of dollars into poorer countries, with research and delivery initiatives focusing on agricultural improvement, sanitation, nutrition, immunisation, malaria control and more. Many entrepreneurs promote higher learning and research, not in pursuit of commercial benefits to themselves, but because cutting-edge science and technology excites them. That might explain why so many of today's super-entrepreneurs are fascinated with space exploration—something far too risky to be explained as a straightforward commercial project.

And over the decades and centuries, entrepreneurs have been disproportionately responsible for radical innovations that have changed people's lives on a massive scale. These innovations include things like the printing press; steam engines; carding, spinning and weaving machines; the telephone; railroads; gramophones; aeroplanes; float glass; and home computers. Indeed, the list is endless. Often the inventors were looking for something else when they chanced on their discovery, as with the microwave oven, or penicillin, even Corn Flakes and Super Glue. Occasionally they have sparked the creation of entire new industries, modernised entire economies and changed our lives and culture.

The social role of profit

Most entrepreneurs may be motivated by the prospect of personal financial gain, but that does not mean that they can succeed only by robbing others. On the contrary, in an open and competitive economy, they can make money only by delivering value to others. Their financial reward comes only through customers, whose lives are improved by their products, and who think the voluntary exchange of money for those products is a fair one. And in that process, entrepreneurs spread value through the population, from which everyone gains.

Remember that *profit* does not mean only *financial* profit. An entrepreneur's customers profit in that they receive a product that they value more than the money they pay for it. Profit simply means getting more value out than the value you put in—like turning useless and valueless sand into useful, productive and valuable computer chips. Profit is not something to decry but something to celebrate on account of its economic and social benefits. If we can use fewer resources to create more value, after all, we are all made better off.

Inasmuch as entrepreneurs pursue *financial* profit—earning more money from a venture than the amount they spend on materials and manufacturing—that profit motive has the positive social effect of boosting value, widening choice and improving products for everyone. Indeed, the bigger the profit, the bigger the general social gain is likely to be. Financial profit is a rough indicator of the additional value that the entrepreneur creates. It shows that the entrepreneur has found a way to reduce cost—allowing expensive resources to be redirected to more productive uses—and increase the value produced by supplying cheaper, more plentiful or better-quality products to willing purchasers. Indeed, the more open and competitive the economy, and the easier it is for competitors to enter and leave the market, the greater is the pressure on entrepreneurs to keep on reducing input costs and raising product value. If they slack off, after all, others will gladly step in to capture the reward.

The result, once again, is a continual improvement in productivity and value creation. As that improvement goes on, things that were once luxuries and affordable only by the few—fresh meat, running water, domestic heating, electricity, cars, washing machines, computers—become better and cheaper. Access to them spreads out through the community, like ripples on a pond. Cheaper products mean that everyone has more to spend on things they value more; improving quality means that everyone gets more value for the same cost.

We can thank entrepreneurs for such improvements. They may well profit financially from it, but we all gain in other ways. They may even come by their financial profit more by good luck than by shrewd judgement and hard work, but the social benefit is the same.

In fact, it is hard to distinguish how much luck and how much judgement and effort go into any entrepreneur's success. Even good luck has to be grasped and channelled productively if it is to be turned into a profit. Many people envy the 'windfall gains' that come through good luck, and even demand that they should be taxed; but the only effect of that is to reduce the number of entrepreneurs on the alert for missed opportunities—to the detriment and loss of the whole society. Society would be better off if we encouraged more people to think and act entrepreneurially and allowed those who did to enjoy the rewards of their value creation.

6

The spread of entrepreneurship

Global presence

It is difficult to measure the amount of entrepreneurship that can be found around the world. The obvious indicators such as self-employment or start-up rates are of little use, as we have seen. And even the definition of what should count as 'entrepreneurship' is controversial. It is a matter of opinion whether entrepreneurship is a strictly commercial activity, or whether 'social entrepreneurship' and other forms should be counted. At its widest, everyone is to some extent an entrepreneur, constantly using their skills, abilities and resources to create the greatest value for themselves at the lowest cost of time, money and effort. On that score, entrepreneurial activity can be found in every part of the globe.

But the same is true of commercial entrepreneurship. It exists in every country—rich, average or poor. It abounds in the US and Norway as it does in Turkey or South Africa and Angola or Guatemala. There is entrepreneurial spirit even in non-market economies—though much of it aims at getting around official controls through bribery or black-market trading. While the daily 'ballot' of open markets is much more efficient, such illegal markets work in much the same way to plug shortages and co-ordinate supply and demand. The difference is that their entrepreneurs must be prepared to break the law.

Country similarities and differences

Though entrepreneurship exists everywhere, some countries stand out. Some, for example, produce large numbers of billionaire super-entrepreneurs, which might indicate that they are good places for entrepreneurship in general. Hong Kong, Israel, the United States, Switzerland, Singapore, Norway, Ireland, Taiwan, Canada and Australia lead the field. Such countries have open values and institutions that encourage success, making people believe that they *can* succeed and be rewarded for their efforts. They also have a shared commitment to the rule of law, limited government and strong property rights, suggesting that these factors are also important.

Most, in addition, have a legal system that allows entrepreneurs to experiment without requiring some authority's permission. This again may explain why they are more entrepreneurial (in the case of the US, several times more entrepreneurial) than most continental countries in Europe, where specific rules, rather than general principles, determine what activities are permissible. As the American economist Adam Thierer points out, the US abounds with innovative companies that grew up there: Microsoft, Yahoo, YouTube, Amazon, Google, PayPal, Twitter, Dropbox, Facebook, Snapchat; but it is difficult to name more than one or two comparable European innovators. He attributes this difference to America's 'permissionless innovation'—where no permits are needed to launch an innovation—in contrast to continental Europe's completely opposite approach to change.[40]

"If we spend all our time living in constant fear of worst-case scenarios—and premising public policy upon such fears—it means that best-case scenarios will never come about. Wisdom and progress are born from experience, including experiences that involve risk and the possibility of occasional mistakes and failures."

—Adam Thierer, *Permissionless Innovation*

Culture is plainly important too. Perhaps the culture of the entrepreneur-producing countries is more welcoming and less hostile to personal success, encouraging individual ambition. But poorer and less liberal countries share some of those values too. People in the Middle East and North Africa tell surveys that they think becoming an entrepreneur is a good career move, while those in the Caribbean and Latin America see being an entrepreneur as high status. Latin Americans also seem to have little fear of failure, and indeed entrepreneurship is strongest where business failures are highest—which suggests that a cultural acceptance of failure may encourage people to take risks and grasp potential opportunities.[41]

40 Thierer, A. (2014) *Permissionless Innovation: The Continuing Case for Comprehensive Technological Freedom. Global Entrepreneurship Monitor.* Arlington Virginia: Mercatus Center at George Mason University.

41 *Ibid.*

There are other interesting findings. Most entrepreneurs are men—though there is more gender equality on this score in the more advanced trading nations. Middle Eastern and North African countries score highly on *international* entrepreneurship, perhaps because of their geographical position astride trade routes. In China, entrepreneurial activity grew after the death of Mao but now seems to be flattening out. In the US, by contrast, entrepreneurship declined after the 2008 financial crisis, but soon rebounded. But it is hard to measure these trends with much precision.

Developing countries

Developing countries may not seem ideal places for entrepreneurship. Individuals and their families are less likely to have savings that could be used to establish and expand new businesses. The local banking and financial sectors may not be very advanced, nor well-funded. International capital suppliers may not understand local conditions and may be wary of what they find. Management skills and education may be poor. Infrastructure and distribution networks may be crude.

Yet they have advantages too. For example, developing countries have lower living costs; so there are opportunities for providing services, such as call centres, accountancy, internet and other back-office functions, to businesses and individuals in richer countries. Access to cheap and simple technology may provide a stronger boost to productivity than it does in economies that are already well developed: smartphones allowing the instant communication of prices to local traders, for example, or IT fuelling the creation of completely new industries.

Since a number of sectors in a developing country may be not fully mature, there is also more scope for diversification than in a developed country, where markets and the businesses that serve them are more specialised. That potential allows entrepreneurs in developing countries to spread risk by running enterprises with multiple, though often complementary, functions such as mining, cement and construction.

Another potential advantage for entrepreneurs in developing countries is that the opportunities are more general. As Kirzner might say, there is more that is yet to be discovered and less that has been discovered already. There are also likely to be more market opportunities that are not already filled by other entrepreneurs, as might quickly happen in a richer country with greater access to capital.

Entrepreneurship and migration

Another discovery that emerges from any global survey of entrepreneurship is that being open to foreign talent is particularly important. A review of the evidence by The Entrepreneurs Network showed that while just one in seven (14%) of UK residents were foreign-born, nearly half (49%) of the UK's fast-growing start-ups had at least one foreign-born co-founder, coming from 29 different countries as diverse as the US, Germany, Russia, India, Australia, Mexico and Vietnam. Immigrants were one-and-a-half times more likely to start, own and run a business than people born in the UK.[42]

One reason for this might be that many immigrants are natural entrepreneurs, having already grappled with risk and uncertainty by moving to a different country, often with no friends or family there to help them. Their willingness to move to a new life shows that they have courage and ambition. Immigrants are also more likely to be young and energetic. Once relocated, they see their adopted country differently

42 Dumitriu, S. and A. Stewart (2019).

from the locals, and are more willing to question how it works and more able to see the opportunities that might come through changes. For example, they may spot market inefficiencies and shortages that the locals regard as natural.

Cultural minorities often lead entrepreneurial development. Being more on the margins of the society, with different ways of thinking and perhaps less to lose, they may be more able and willing than the locals to make creative adjustments to changing events. They are perhaps more likely to try solutions that challenge the prevailing culture and class system, but which nevertheless work better than others. They may even see changes happening earlier and more clearly than the natives do, giving them the advantage of moving ahead of the crowd.

For these and other reasons, migrants into the UK and US (and probably many other countries) are more likely to start their own businesses than the native citizens. Fully half of the engineering and tech companies in Silicon Valley, for instance, have immigrant founders—including Google, Facebook and Tesla. Of the companies in the 2017 *Fortune 500* list, 43% were founded by an immigrant or the child of an immigrant, including Apple, Amazon, Boeing, General Electric, Verizon, J P Morgan and even Ford.

Industries suited to entrepreneurship

Some industries seem more suited to entrepreneurial action, others less. In particular, entrepreneurs are found predominantly in sectors that have lower start-up capital needs, including internet and data services (e.g. sharing apps, software and cybersecurity), investment advice, consulting and accountancy services. That may be no surprise: plainly it is harder for an entrepreneur to establish a new business where capital costs are high (e.g. car making, shipbuilding, airlines, healthcare and energy), though some do. Most of today's super-entrepreneurs and fastest-growing companies are to be found in IT, biotech, finance and retail. They are also more likely to be found in businesses that can be leveraged to create a large fast-growing firm, such as hedge funds and social media.

In poorer countries, according to the *Global Entrepreneurship Monitor*, entrepreneurs are found most often in sales businesses, such as commodities, wholesale and retail. In richer countries, they cluster in finance, property and business services. Among entrepreneurial enterprises globally, the proportion of wholesale and retail businesses has shrunk while the proportion of services and technology companies has grown. That may simply indicate that the world is getting richer and that there is growing demand for services that were once luxuries, if they existed at all. Or it may be that people in many formerly poor countries have now built up sufficient capital to branch out of staple sectors and explore more sophisticated ones, which (like IT services) can be marketed and sold worldwide. For example, South Korea—one of the world's poorest countries in the 1950s but now one of the richest—is particularly strong on 'gig economy' entrepreneurship. Perhaps this sector will be home to a growing proportion of the world's future super-entrepreneurs.

Intrapreneurship, where entrepreneurial innovation comes from within already established companies, seems to be strongest in Europe, where Sweden, Germany and Cyprus have a particularly large role. This may be due to institutions and structures (such as tax and corporate governance laws, regulatory burdens or bank and bond financing as opposed to share ownership) that favour large companies over start-ups. People of entrepreneurial spirit might then find satisfaction with much less risk by working in larger companies.

The future of entrepreneurship

As mentioned earlier, some Western observers believe they see a large fall in business dynamism over time. A Brookings Institution survey of research on the subject points to the downward trend in the rate of new business start-ups in the US, together with a declining rate at which existing firms drop out of markets. At the same time, the share of US employment generated by younger firms has dropped. Since the 1980s, the share of workers employed in start-ups has fallen from 20 percent to 10 percent, while the share employed by larger, mature firms has risen from 40 percent to 50 percent.[43]

These are imperfect indicators, and if there is indeed a decline in business dynamism, it could be local, temporary or due to many different factors, such as low interest rates helping unproductive 'zombie' companies to stay alive. Overall, however, the evidence does suggest that productivity growth is falling in the US, UK, Germany and other developed economies, and that falling business dynamism is a major reason.

So why this decline? Again, there are alternative explanations.[44] Some people argue that the lower population growth in advanced economies may mean there is a smaller pool of potential entrepreneurs[45]—though that should matter little if they still start up in the most productive sectors. Others say that the rising importance of branding and of costly IT systems makes it harder for start-ups to compete (think of global

....

43 Decker, R. A., Haltiwanger, J., et al. (2016).

44 Dumitriu, S. (2019) 'What's Really Driving Our Productivity Slump?' *CapX,* July 5.

45 Hathaway, I. and R. Litan. (2014) 'What's driving the decline in the firm formation rate? A partial Explanation.' *Brookings Institution*, Brookings Economic Studies, November.

search engines, office software or online shopping platforms).[46] But in fact the gains from scale have not risen much, and if anything IT has significantly cut the costs faced by many small businesses.[47]

A more likely culprit, linked to size, is regulation. Regulations on products (e.g. labelling rules), processes (e.g. manufacturing methods) or employment (e.g. minimum wages, working hours, parental leave) impose a greater burden on small businesses than on large ones. Large firms can spread the cost of compliance over a large number of sales; small start-ups cannot. That may be why large increases in regulation, such as America's 2010 Dodd-Frank controls on financial services firms, seem to boost profit margins in the larger firms.[48] Likewise, we find that regulated economies, such as South Korea, Taiwan, Hong Kong, Thailand and Singapore, have growing numbers of entrepreneurs and super-entrepreneurs. In highly regulated Europe, by contrast, innovation is more likely to come through *intrapreneurship* within large companies.

"Regulation may be actively sought by an industry, or it may be thrust upon it. ...as a rule, regulation is acquired by the industry and is designed and operated primarily for its benefit."

—George Stigler,

'The Theory of Economic Regulation', Bell Journal of Economics and Management Science, Vol 2 No 1 (1971)

....

46 De Ridder, M. (2019), 'Market Power and Innovation in the Intangible Economy.' *Centre for Macroeconomics*, Discussion Paper.

47 Gutiérrez, G. and T. Philippon. (2019) 'The Failure of Free Entry.' *National Bureau of Economic Research*, Working Paper 26001, June.

48 *Ibid.*

Large firms can also afford more lobbyists, on whom legislators necessarily rely for specialist information as the regulatory issues become ever more complex. But those lobbyists have an interest in keeping competitors out; and if they can force start-up entrepreneurs to spend their energy, not on creating more attractive products, but on dealing with onerous regulation, that interest is served.

The public's interests, however, are better served and protected by an open, dynamic, competitive industry than a heavily regulated, lethargic, unresponsive one. Policies such as the UK Financial Conduct Authority's 'regulatory sandbox', which allows fintech start-ups to experiment with new business models without the threat of regulatory sanctions, would seem a step in the right direction.

7

Productive and unproductive entrepreneurship

Is entrepreneurship always productive?

Being alert to opportunities that might benefit us, and acting upon them, seem natural and universal human characteristics. Back in 1776, Adam Smith noted the "uniform, constant and uninterrupted effort of every man to better his condition," and argued that "the propensity to truck, barter and exchange one thing for another" was "one of those original principles in human nature" that needed no explanation.[49] And through the "higgling and bargaining of the market" our self-interest would—surprisingly—produce mutual benefit, as if "led by an invisible hand."

In open and competitive markets, it might. But life affords many other opportunities for people to better themselves, though not always for mutual benefit. Clever lawyers may exploit legal loopholes that get their clients off speeding fines, for example, without generating any value for society. Thieves and fraudsters may be just as alert to criminal opportunities as any entrepreneur is to honest ones. The

49 Smith (1776).

difference is that their grasping of those criminal opportunities does not create value but takes value from others.

Productive, unproductive and destructive

So, it is clear that not all 'entrepreneurship' is productive and socially beneficial. Indeed, entrepreneurship can be *productive*, *unproductive* or *destructive* according to Baumol.[50] There are no clear boundaries, but one might say that the *productive* sort creates value all round, the *unproductive* sort generates value for one side only, and the *destructive* sort actually destroys value.

Productive entrepreneurship. *Productive* entrepreneurs create value for both themselves and their customers. Value is in the eye of the beholder. The customers value the entrepreneur's product more than the cash they pay for it; the entrepreneurs value the price they receive more than the resources (e.g. time, effort and materials) that they have to spend on supplying the product. The relationship is entirely voluntary: either could walk away from the deal, but they do not because they consider themselves made better off by the exchange. They might each trade only for reasons of self-interest—the customer wanting the product, the producer wanting the money. But the process creates a much more general benefit. In the process of pursuing custom, productive entrepreneurs innovate, raise productivity, advance progress, expand our choices, boost our value and ultimately benefit the whole society.

....

50 Baumol, W. (1990) 'Entrepreneurship: Productive, Unproductive and Destructive.' In *Journal of Political Economy* 98(5), Part 1, October.

Unproductive entrepreneurship. Then again, one can be entrepreneurial without creating value for anyone else. Another common example is tax avoidance, where alert taxpayers and their advisers look for (legal) opportunities to reduce their tax bill by 'creative' accounting measures. They might put money into tax-aided retirement schemes rather than take it as income. They might quit as an employee and set up a company to provide the same services, allowing them to claim write-offs or exploit business subsidies. Or they might reduce their company's tax liability by funnelling profits from high-tax to low-tax countries—as Starbucks, Apple, Amazon, Netflix and General Motors have all been accused of—or by relocating their headquarters to a low-tax jurisdiction.

Another example is lobbying in order to get regulations and regulatory decisions made in your favour. That might involve convincing politicians to keep the tax or trading rules favourable to your business sector, for example, or befriending officials in the hope that they might be more inclined to grant a trading licence or building permit. As government power has expanded, lobbying has grown into a huge industry, with US companies (led by pharmaceuticals, insurance, electronics, oil and utilities) spending over $3 billion a year on it.[51] There may be no identifiable victims who lose out from this self-promotion, but the lobbyists must clearly think it benefits them massively.

Destructive entrepreneurship. However, some other entrepreneurial activities—if they can really be called that—certainly do have victims.

The American economist Gary Becker (1930-2014) argued that

51 Evers-Hillstrom, Karl (2018) 'Lobbying Spending Reaches $3.4 billion in 2018, highest in 8 years.' *OpenSecrets: Center for Responsive Politics*, January 25.

criminals act much like honest entrepreneurs, assessing the potential reward and probability of succeeding, against the risk of being caught and punished.[52] Alert to opportunities to rob or cheat others, they may use blackmail or run scams and rackets. They may threaten businesses with violence if they do not pay protection money.

These are not voluntary transactions: they take value from victims without their willing consent. The wider such exploitation spreads, the greater the destruction: including less choice and freedom, lower productivity, and the loss of value to society.

The crucial effect of rules

Whether a particular entrepreneurial action is productive, unproductive or destructive can depend on the rules that are in place.

For example, not all illegal activity is necessarily destructive. It does not seem destructive to offer a terminally ill patient some medicine that could potentially save them but has not yet completed the official bureaucratic approval process. Or again, only authoritarian regimes suffer when a dealer secretly supplies customers with books that have been banned. Such transactions are mindful and voluntary, and nobody else is affected.

Equally, some legal activity may be destructive. A doctor, for example, may perform profitable but unnecessary operations by exploiting patients' lack of full knowledge about their medical condition. The patient may consent to the operation, but it is not necessarily *informed* consent.

The specific laws and regulations that are in place can make a big difference to whether entrepreneurial energy streams into productive

....

52 Becker, G. (1968) 'Crime and Punishment: An Economic Approach.' In *Journal of Political Economy* 76: 169-217.

purposes or into unproductive and destructive ones. If taxes are high and complicated, for example, a great deal of entrepreneurial ingenuity will be focused on (legally) avoiding them or (illegally) evading them, rather than on creating value by supplying better and cheaper products. If employment tribunals are costless for workers but can award big pay-outs from employers, workers will be prompted to make vexatious claims and employers' energy will be diverted into avoiding them. If regulations threaten profitability, energy will be directed into circumventing them or lobbying to get them changed. Likewise, if particular activities are subsidised, people will concoct ways to capture the subsidy—whether or not they serve its intention.

Manipulating the rules

The sad result of burdensome or inept laws, regulations, grants and subsidies is that business entrepreneurs can often make more money—or avoid huge costs—by hiring lawyers, accountants and lobbyists rather than engineers, designers, managers and other productive workers. Manipulating the rules—by lobbying, court action, financing favourable politicians or even bribing officials—can be very profitable, which is why so much energy is spent on it.

Even in Ancient Rome, the way to riches was power and influence rather than trade and commerce—on which those with power and influence looked down. Emperors granted their allies and favourites exclusive monopolies, even over essentials such as construction, shipping, salt and mining. A thousand years later, England's medieval guilds prevailed on their cronies in government to restrict the number of apprentices entering their trade and banning competitors coming in from other towns. Merchants, farmers and manufacturers lobbied monarchs for protection against 'unfair' competition, such as cheap grain or printed calico; even a new labour-saving stocking-frame was banned. As in Rome, royal charters granted monopolies to individuals and companies.

Such privileges benefited only the fortunate producers, at the expense of the general public. They were not just unproductive, but destructive: they denied entrepreneurial opportunity to others, suppressed innovation, reduced productivity, forced the public to pay higher prices and accept lower quality, and further diverted talent into the exploitation of power rather than the creation of value. But when, in England, royal patronage, grants and monopolies were eventually scaled back in the seventeenth and eighteenth centuries, there were fewer rewards to be had from cronyism. As a result, entrepreneurial attention turned from unproductive to productive uses, stimulating innovation, agricultural improvement and a snowballing industrial revolution.

Occupational licensing

Nevertheless, unproductive and destructive entrepreneurship are far from dead. The American economist Milton Friedman (1912-2006) reviewed the occupational licensing of professional people such as doctors and accountants.[53] Though this was supposed to protect the public, Friedman found that it had the opposite effect. Licensing allowed professionals to charge higher fees, and deliver an inferior service, by restricting the numbers of people who were permitted to practice. Today, occupational licensing is even more widespread than when Friedman wrote. It is estimated that half the professions in the US require a licence, including hairdressers, funeral directors, interior

....

53 Friedman, M. (1962) *Capitalism and Freedom*. University of Chicago Press, Ch 9.

designers, jockeys and manicurists. That allows huge numbers of professionals to protect themselves from competition. (All the more so when it is those in the profession who decide what the rules should be, as doctors and lawyers do, for example.) And it becomes harder for outsiders to break into the market—particularly poorer people who may not be able to afford the necessary fees and requirements.

An example is the North Carolina teeth-whitening scandal. Whitening teeth is a fairly simple process. You take little plastic trays, pour some fluid in them, then place them against the client's teeth. No major training is required. But as teeth-whitening clinics started springing up in shopping malls and salons, licensed dentists—who charged far more—objected. They got the licensing board to issue cease-and-desist orders telling the clinics to stop their unauthorised 'dentistry'. Because the established dentists dominated the licensing board, while the clinics were unrepresented, they could use the board's official powers to stifle competition and consumer choice.[54]

Licences to operate taxis are common across the world. Again, the justification is that this gives passengers greater security by ensuring that operators are 'fit and proper' persons; but the effect is to restrict the number of operators and raise prices. In 1937, for example, New York—under pressure from taxi drivers who found it hard to attract customers in the post-Depression years and who were undercut by 'wildcats'—stopped issuing any new licences. Today, there are just 13,500—two-thirds of the 1930s peak, even though the demand for cabs has soared. But owners of these 'medallions' (who rent them out to drivers by the hour) like it that way. Only now are innovative

....

54 NPR (2018) 'Rigging the economy', No. 829, March 9.

ride-sharing apps breaking into taxi markets; but they are resisted by the established providers, who are often represented on the licensing authorities, as the 'black cabs' are in London, for instance. Hence, ride-sharing apps, which offer lower prices and an arguably superior service, have often been forced out. France even put Uber executives in prison, such is the lobbying influence of incumbent businesses over politicians.

Much regulation is instigated by large established businesses, who promote it as protecting the public, but who (consciously or unconsciously) stand to benefit from its dampening effect on competition. Operating rules such as minimum capital requirements, minimum and maximum price laws, and rigidly specified product standards or processes all make it difficult for entrepreneurial start-ups to provide cheaper, innovative products. Indeed, even establishing what the regulations *are* can be a costly exercise for a small challenger business. Larger firms can more easily afford legal challenges to make life difficult for new firms that are taking their customers; and they can spend more on lobbying and developing crony relationships with regulators to help them distort regulatory decisions in their favour and against their competitors.

The rise of political entrepreneurship

It is true that unregulated businesses might produce harmful social outcomes, such as misleading offers to customers, poor production and quality standards, one-sided contracts or unsafe working conditions. But then bad customer reviews (particularly in the online age) drive out firms with poor practices and products. And in any case, most entrepreneurs want to create superior, innovative products that their customers love and value. The greater danger is undoubtedly over-regulation, and the tendency for regulation to grow under the pressure of the larger producers who benefit from it. That expansion of regulation makes it harder for new firms to grow and prosper, locks us into old technologies, holds back economic progress and encourages yet more cronyism.

It is the same the world over. The *chaebol* of South Korea benefited from government regulations and subsidies and drove the South Korean economy for years—until their bribery and corruption were exposed. Oligarchs in Russia grew rich through their political patronage, but ordinary Russians derived scant value from their activities. A survey of entrepreneurs in Poland revealed that they focused more on unproductive activities than productive ones.[55] Elsewhere in Eastern Europe the story is much the same. Companies in the US not only spend billions on lobbying: they also pay large sums to get ex-regulators and ex-ministers on their boards. Government power attracts those who would exploit it.

Arguably, the slow economic growth rates in many of the most developed countries like the US and Europe, are not due to a shortage of entrepreneurship and the falling rate of business start-ups. It is because entrepreneurial energy has shifted from productive activities and into unproductive ones; from creating better and cheaper products and into lobbying, cronyism and litigation. Individual self-interest benefits society only if the institutions are aligned positively. If they are not, then even rich countries decline as a result of cronyism and the rise of unproductive activity—as Ancient Rome and Ancient China did centuries ago.

55 Dominiak, P. and Wasilczuk, J. (2017) 'Formal Institutions: The Source of Unproductive Entrepreneurship in Poland.' GUT FME Working Paper Series A, 1/2017(44), Gdańsk University of Technology, Faculty of Management and Economics, Gdańsk.

Entrepreneurship and institutions

How then do we create the institutions and incentives to keep entrepreneurism productive? A stable political environment and good access to capital certainly help. Secure property rights, the reliability of the justice system, and limits on political power seem important too.

But creating these conditions is not easy. Old institutions might create perverse incentives and yet be deeply grounded in history, culture and belief systems. Typically, they will be fiercely defended by those who benefit from them, who are often those in authority. Institutional change is therefore not a simple shift to something more logical, as textbook economics might imply. It is political and emotional. When the Berlin Wall fell in 1989, for example, there was a popular mood to shake off the repression of the past. Most Western economists expected market institutions and morality to triumph rapidly. In some places, mostly those where liberal institutions existed before the Soviet era (such as Estonia and the Czech Republic), that did largely happen. But in most, the transition was fraught. Some (such as Ukraine) went one way then the other. Others (like Russia, with no history of market values) never really reformed but engendered a new power class of oligarchs and criminals. Culture, history, religion and the realities of power are strong. The corrupting influence of perverse institutions runs deep.

All too often, the countries in most need of reforms that would redirect entrepreneurs to productive ends never make them, because the ruling authorities fear the impact on their own power. Others may not realise the huge scale of the reforms needed, clinging on to the idea that they can manage markets and dictate output or employment targets. Reform-blocking corruption (even among the police and justice authorities) may be hard to root out. The old destructive entrepreneurism lingers on.

The entrepreneurial spirit is strong and widespread. It is a powerful force for prosperity and progress. But we need to create sound institutions that channel it into socially valuable directions. It is wise not to underestimate the scale of that task.

8

Can government promote entrepreneurship?

Recognising the benefits of entrepreneurship for the economy and society, many governments have tried to develop policy to encourage it. Most fail, usually because they are confused about what they are trying to create, or because their strategies are too short-term, too bureaucratic, too ignorant of market realities or too focused on political rather than economic ends. Government efforts to promote entrepreneurship are, as Harvard economist Josh Lerner put it, a 'Boulevard of Broken Dreams'.[56]

The Boulevard of Broken Dreams

In 2002, for example, the European Union adopted what is now known as the 'Lisbon Strategy.' It maintained that "economic growth and jobs depend upon business and the creative spirit of entrepreneurs," and proposed policy reforms to encourage that spirit. It aimed to make the EU, by 2010, "the most competitive and dynamic knowledge-based

56 Lerner, J. (2009).

economy in the world" through "innovation for growth," "investing in research" and "developing entrepreneurship within a competitive business environment." Well before 2010, however, EU officials were admitting the Strategy to be an abject failure.

Policy failures. Much of the reason was that the Strategy did not distinguish small firms from entrepreneurial firms. It aimed at creating more small and medium-sized enterprises; but as we have seen, that is not the same as entrepreneurship and can even be the exact opposite. Innovative entrepreneurship rates are low in several EU countries, such as Greece, Italy, Spain and Portugal, though self-employment rates are high. Meanwhile the self-employment rate in Silicon Valley, one of the world's most dynamic entrepreneurial clusters, is about half the average in the rest of California.[57]

Grants, subsidies and tax breaks can make self-employment attractive. But policies that promote self-employment may not promote entrepreneurship. Often they merely make unproductive small businesses viable and discourage potential entrepreneurs from expanding. As entrepreneurship experts Tino and Nima Sanandaji put it, "The question should be: 'do we want to have more Googles and Wal-Marts *or* more plumbers and a larger number of independent retail stores?'"[58]

The Strategy also called for EU public research and development spending to rise to 3% of GDP. But there is no clear link between research spending and entrepreneurship. Research is not invention, and invention is not product innovation. Research may provide the

....

57 Sanandaji, T. and Sanandaji, N. (2014).

58 Sanandaji, T. and Leeson, P. (2013).

materials for invention, and inventions may provide the materials for innovative products. But those products must be made viable and attractive if they are to contribute to economic progress and growth, and that takes entrepreneurial skill. No amount of public (or private) spending on research will generate more valued products without the engagement of entrepreneurs.

Lastly, the Lisbon Strategy ignored the crucial impact of economic policy (such as taxes and regulations) on entrepreneurship. Entrepreneurs already face uncertain future returns, and high taxes eat into their potential profits and so greatly increase the risk of the enterprise. Regulations, too, impose a 'time tax' burden that impacts heavily on smaller and growing companies that may not be well organized to deal with them. They may also preclude the use of innovative technologies by specifying old process standards.

Other strategies

When Lerner reviewed various governments' initiatives to boost entrepreneurialism, he discovered most of them are failures—often merely repeating the mistakes of others in the past. For example, many countries have tried to reproduce the entrepreneurial dynamism of Silicon Valley; but nothing on the same scale has ever been achieved. And several other Middle East states have tried to replicate the huge success of Dubai, which turned its natural harbour into a massive freeport trading centre. They all ended up out of pocket. Clearly, it is not easy to create new entrepreneurial hubs where none exist. Their success often turns on a peculiar mixture of geography, circumstances and people.

Entrepreneurial government. Governments have also tried to make their civil service 'entrepreneurial', though these efforts usually fail too. In the early 2000s, Britain's Prime Minister, Tony Blair, called for an "entrepreneurial civil service" but as the Easyjet entrepreneur Stelios Haji-Ioannou told him: "You can't have an entrepreneurial civil service because you don't have any competition." Without competition, and the prospect of great reward for great success, public servants are unlikely to turn into public entrepreneurs. A House of Commons Committee was still yearning for "a more innovative and entrepreneurial civil service" a decade later.[59]

Competition is important because, if customers cannot realistically move to another supplier, then there is little incentive on a monopoly service, public or private, to search for better and cheaper ways to produce better and cheaper offerings. This is compounded by the fact that individual civil servants themselves cannot really profit from successful innovations. At best they might be promoted, but they can never expect the kinds of fortunes that commercial entrepreneurs dream of. They are more likely to get blamed and lose promotion if a project goes wrong. As a result, their motivation to innovate and take risks is limited. Their key priority is to 'cover their backs' by eliminating as much risk from projects as possible.

Taking risks with public money is controversial anyway. National and local governments that make disastrous investments are roundly denounced, but there is usually little praise for them when investments go well. Indeed, the civil service is tied down by rules that are designed purposefully to prevent them putting public money at great risk. And civil servants themselves are not generally risk-takers: they may well

59 UK Government. (2011) 'Change in Government: the Agenda for Leadership.' House of Commons: Public Administration Select Committee: Report 13, Session 2010-2012.

choose their occupation precisely because they value security instead.

Why politicians get involved

Some of the reasons why politicians attempt to stimulate entrepreneurship have been outlined already: the advantages of innovation, value enhancement, productivity, progress, economic growth, employment, product improvement and social benefits among them. Also, as one product development leads to another, it sets off snowballing improvement and value enhancement throughout the whole community. It is therefore obvious why governments might want to encourage entrepreneurs and promote entrepreneurship.

Governments might also believe it to be a matter of national prestige to have a lively entrepreneurial sector, particularly one involved in leading-edge technologies like artificial intelligence or sustainable energy. They might think that these leading industries can be accelerated if government can provide a bridge between entrepreneurs and sources of development capital, and that this would generate further gains for the wider community. With the same intention, they may even aim to provide development capital themselves. Governments may feel that, while start-up entrepreneurs might know all about the technology they are pioneering, they may not be so good at running a business, nor convincing others to fund them, so they need information and advice or even help in negotiating contracts with private capital providers. Governments may also believe that they can provide a bridge between international capital and local entrepreneurs—not only introducing them to foreign capital providers (which few start-ups think about) but in helping streamline the logistics and reducing the paperwork involved in matching the two up.

Government may see such help as benefiting both current and future generations and creating a more diversified and stronger economy. They may also consider that having a high rate of entrepreneurship and innovation is a mark of national prestige and that some official endorsement will help to indicate that they want to encourage innovation and want entrepreneurs to be taken more seriously. Or they may think that the pioneering 'first movers' in any new business sector have to struggle and spend more time and energy on research and development than those who follow and copy them, though the social benefit from building on a pioneer's efforts is considerable. So, they may want to give aid to pioneers in order to encourage more innovative thinking in order to boost the social benefits that result.

Public investment vehicles

With all this in mind, many governments have invested massively in trying to promote entrepreneurship. Many countries have 'sovereign funds' or 'social wealth funds'—state-owned investment funds that invest in financial assets such as stocks and bonds, gold or foreign exchange, private equity and hedge funds. They are often set up as holding companies for strategic investments such as aviation or utility businesses, or to build up long-term capital for future generations (often, like Norway, from the revenues of oil or some other national commodity assets with a finite life). Commodity-based countries may also use them to help smooth revenues when commodity prices fluctuate, though the general aim is not to use them to pay for unsustainable public spending—and indeed to prevent 'windfall' revenues being frittered away.

Such funds can be used to promote research, development, education and other spending that is believed to boost entrepreneurship. But being large and powerful, they can also distort markets and crowd out private entrepreneurship finance. They may also be very bureaucratic, not very transparent and have vague and uncertain aims: not just to make a profit, as a private fund might aim for, but to serve undefined and changeable political objectives too. The same problems also apply to other public investments that may be intended to promote entrepreneurship, such as subsidies, grants, infrastructure projects and tax breaks. Often, as with the Lisbon Strategy, governments cannot even clearly define what the 'entrepreneurship' they are trying to promote actually is, nor measure their success in achieving it.

For and against government intervention

Given all this, it should be no surprise that most such government efforts to promote entrepreneurship are failures, with few obvious benefits to show in terms of boosting innovation and enterprise. Yet many supporters of such intervention question whether things can simply be left to the market.

Government and IT. For example, Silicon Valley, they argue, was not a product of pure market capitalism. There were plenty of government loans and subsidies for IT initiatives, and defence and other government projects gave IT entrepreneurs the money to start up and grow their businesses. Stanford University may have been private, but by the 1950s it was the best place to find researchers who could help the military and intelligence services meet the challenges of the Cold War, and NASA to win the Space Race. The US government became its biggest customer. And out of those contracts sprang firms making IT hardware and software. Only when New York investors started to see what was happening did 'risk capital' funds start to come in.[60]

In addition, the government largely shaped the markets that Silicon Valley's leading IT firms now operate in. The internet, after all, started as a military communications project, then expanded into academe, and only then onto our home computers. Global Positioning by Satellite (GPS), once again was led by government. Google's search algorithm was funded by government grants; Windows, Google Maps, the Cloud and video-conferencing were all given a crucial start by government. Tesla got a half-billion-dollar loan from the US Department of Energy, and other Elon Musk industries received nearly five billion dollars in public support.[61] Even the patent system under which Silicon Valley companies protect their inventions is a government construct. The idea that Silicon Valley is a product of free-market enterprise, say the critics, is just wrong and is an excuse to lobby for lower taxes and easier regulations.

The case against. Against all this is the point that promoting economic enterprise is not the core business of government, nor even an endeavour that it is either good or competent at. Other countries such as France have tried to reproduce Silicon Valley and create their own technology clusters; but like that attempt, the usual result is a large expenditure of taxpayers' money for no obvious gain. Private venture capitalists scrutinise and assess the prospects of start-up companies every day, have the experience and know-how to do so, and the incentive to move quickly and get the decisions right. Civil servants, by contrast,

....

60 Medairos, J. and Mazzucato, M. (2019) 'This Economist has a Plan to Fix Capitalism. It's Time we all Listened.' Wired, October 8.

61 Ibid.

are generally over-stretched and more focused on political issues than profit. Seeking to achieve particular public policy objectives, they tend to over-engineer their support programmes with that in mind, whether or not it makes business sense.

They also lack the skill and experience to review potential investments as thoroughly as venture capitalists do. They have little awareness of how large or small their support should be in order to deliver the most good, so public money is either wasted, or is given in too small doses to make a real difference. And crucially, civil servants are over-optimistic: they rarely expect their investments to fail, even though most start-ups do.

The incentive structures of governments and businesspeople do not match either. Entrepreneurs, focusing on the long-term value of their enterprise, work on long lead times and develop products and processes that may take years, even decades, to pay off. Politicians rarely look far beyond the next electoral cycle. They want to give out cash quickly to prospective entrepreneurial businesses, hoping for equally quick successes that they can point to when they next face the electorate. But in that rush, there can be little careful focus on the structure, strengths and weaknesses of these firms, or the potential of the market they work in, or what their real needs are, or what terms and conditions are best applied to any government support.

Governments can also be captured, and government programmes gamed, leading again to bad investment decisions and counterproductive results. As far back as 1776, when the British government provided a subsidy ('bounty') to fishing fleets based on the size of the vessels, Adam Smith complained that it was "too common for vessels to fit out for the sole purpose of catching, not the fish, but the bounty." Pork-barrel legislation, where representatives try to skew government spending towards their own district, is also common and does not promote good decisions. The job-creation motive also sees money spent on make-work projects rather than on the effective promotion of enterprises. Grants and subsidies that are meant for small- and medium-sized enterprises are grasped by the larger players, who can afford to engage dedicated teams to lobby and apply for them and manage all the reporting that goes with such schemes. Cronyism merely compounds the imbalance. And where the government does admit that it needs professional input to make decisions about which enterprises should be helped, a great part of the budget often ends up in the consultants' hands rather than those of the intended beneficiaries.

Doubters also ask why government capital is even needed. Recent decades have seen a rapid expansion of the private venture capital industry—investors willing to take a substantial risk in providing capital to potentially fast-growing young enterprises, in exchange for large returns, which often includes a stake in the business. The venture capital industry is now global; so, can a national government really make a difference, rather than just getting in the way?

The evidence is that young firms that are backed by private venture capital funds perform better than others. Strikingly, nearly two-thirds (63%) of entrepreneurial companies that are successful enough to make it to an Initial Public Offering in the US come from the tiny number (0.1%) that are venture-capital funded.[62] That may be because venture capitalists devote a huge amount of time and effort on closely scrutinising the firms that they ultimately invest in, are closely involved in the management of those firms, and maintain rigorous and continuing

62 Sanandaji, T. and Sanandaji, N. (2014).

monitoring of their performance. It may be unsurprising that entrepreneurs who do not have that sort of scrutiny, assistance and monitoring may not perform so well. Nor that governments do not perform these tasks well either.

> *"There is always a critical job to be done. There is a sales door to be opened, a credit line to be established, a new important employee to be found, or a business technique to be learned. The venture investor must always be on call to advise, to persuade, to dissuade, to encourage, but always to help build. Then venture capital becomes true creative capital - creating growth for the company and financial success for the investing organization."*

—Georges Doriot, venture capitalist

Setting the right climate

Having looked at many government efforts to promote entrepreneurship, Lerner concludes that the most important thing is to recognise that entrepreneurship needs the right economic and policy environment if it is to thrive.

The right environment. Literacy and school education seem to be some of the most important factors in promoting entrepreneurship. Education gives people ideas and provides them with the basic skills required to deal with others, run a business and manage money. It may also be useful in some cases to have a local academic, scientific and research base, generating knowledge and ideas that attract innovators and provide the raw material that entrepreneurs can turn into practical applications—much as Stanford University did for Silicon Valley.

Flexible labour markets are also important. If regulations make it costly to hire and fire people, employers will hire cautiously, and employees will stick in the same job too long. If, by contrast, people can and do move easily from one job to another, they are more likely to find the job they are best suited for and rising entrepreneurs will find it easier to attract the specific talent they need. A flexible property market, too, enables workers to move between jobs and allows enterprising new firms to move and cluster in places where they can all benefit from sharing ideas and talent.

Entrepreneurship is also boosted by having global standards for both government and business activity, which makes it easier to attract investment from other parts of the world.[63] Of course, there must also be a willingness to accept international investment without bureaucratic strings—such as what industries foreigners can invest in, or how much or how little they can invest, or pointless and invasive paperwork (all of which are too common in many countries). There must also be a rule of law so that contracts can be enforced through an independent judicial process, again encouraging foreigners to risk their capital on promising enterprises. And product markets must be open so that entrepreneurs can benefit from being able to market their products all over the world.

The wrong environment. On the other hand, it is easy to create the wrong political and economic environment for entrepreneurs. Cycles of booms and busts are particularly damaging: they encourage

....

63 Lerner, J. (2009).

over-expansion of businesses in the boom years and then real losses, closures and redundancies when the boom can no longer be sustained. Such cycles are commonly set off by government central banks' over-expansion of money and artificial cheapening of credit—often done deliberately to stimulate a boom. But such artificial booms are invariably followed by a real and costly re-adjustment—rather like the hangover that follows the consumption of an uplifting drug. Entrepreneurs need long-term economic stability if they are going to invest productively and be able to predict future market conditions.

Taxes, regulations, licences and registration requirements that make it harder to start and run companies make it more difficult for entrepreneurs to establish the new enterprises that will deliver their innovations. Likewise, taxes or regulations that favour some companies and sectors over others are also a challenge to entrepreneurs. It is almost always the established firms, with their lobbyists and administrators, who can extract most benefit from such favouritism, not the leaner new start-ups. And again, it is difficult to invest rationally if you cannot predict what type of business some incoming government will favour or turn against.

Governments should also be careful to avoid policies that hamper open bargaining of any kind—between different firms and their suppliers, between firms and financiers or firms and customers, and between employers and employees. As we have seen, 'job protection' measures often serve to protect jobs in outdated industries and starve new enterprises of potential talent. For example, Brazil tried to boost domestic computer hardware manufacture in the 1980s by restricting imports and hindering joint ventures with foreign manufacturers. But this left the country's other businesses paying twice the world price for office equipment that was technologically out of date, hitting Brazil's overall competitiveness.[64]

Similarly, manufacturing standards and marketing regulations are often based on old technologies, effectively outlawing new ones. For example, while vaping and heat-not-burn nicotine products are very much safer than cigarettes and can help smokers to quit, they are often caught by the same restrictions as smoking tobacco.

Through ignorance, it is easy for governments to dislocate the entire market process, and entrepreneurship with it. In today's highly specialised economies, for example, managing the use of resources—which means deciding which of a countless number of resources are best applied in which way to which output in order to maximise value and minimise cost—is a hugely difficult calculation. It can only be solved well when prices are free to move, allowing entrepreneurs to detect which resources and outputs are most valued, and then steering production in that direction. Political interventions that cap prices (common in markets for essential products such as food and utilities) or set minimum wages (common everywhere), have the effect of distorting or suppressing that market price information, making it harder for entrepreneurs to spot surpluses or shortages and re-direct production accordingly.

Most counterproductive policies like these arise from good intentions; but they are easily hijacked by interest groups, including the established industries. Unfortunately, the short-term benefits that such groups might derive from them are far smaller than the long-term and general benefits of a thriving entrepreneurial economy.

....

64 Brooke, J. (1990) 'Brazil Backing Computer Imports.' *The New York Times*, July 9.

"The entrepreneur shifts economic resources out of an area of lower and into an area of higher productivity and greater yield."

—Jean-Baptiste Say, *Traité d'économie politique*

Objective-led encouragement?

Some economists believe that government still has a powerful role in encouraging innovation and entrepreneurship. Instead of focusing on supporting particular businesses or technologies, they say, government should set very broad objectives for society, encouraging innovators to develop their own ways of reaching those ends. Such objectives might include space exploration; developing artificial intelligence or clean energy technology; improving healthcare or food quality and distribution; re-thinking how we live in cities; cleaning up the oceans and much else. Supporters say that such 'management by objectives' works well in business and encourages innovative thinking to solve seemingly difficult management or production problems.[65]

This would be a very different way of encouraging innovation and entrepreneurship and might well avoid the common problems of short-termism, over-prescription, bureaucratic rigidity, inflexible top-down policies, over-optimism and focus on political rather than business objectives. Yet problems remain.

For example, who is to decide these social objectives? One virtue of

65 Medairos, J. and Mazzucato, M. (2019).

the market economy is that individuals decide their own purposes: they do not need politicians and officials to do it for them. Entrepreneurs follow the public's choices—and in a free and open economy, do so very efficiently. Many of the proposed objectives—space exploration, say—might be inspiring, but without detailed cost-benefit analysis how do we know if they are worth the time, money and effort? There may be commercial spin-offs, as there were from the 1960s race to the moon, but we cannot be sure of that (and even in that case, it is questionable whether the spin-offs were worth the huge cost).

There may very well be a case for governments trying to promote innovation; and this objectives-led strategy is at least quite different from the failed old attempts to 'pick winners' among different technologies, sectors or even individual firms. But it is still government that is setting the objectives and deciding what entrepreneurial effort should be focused on, not individual customers. The fact is that these grand objectives are not economic objectives, perhaps not even viable and useful objectives, but merely an unpriced wish-list drawn up by intellectuals and politicians—whose ambitions and choices may be quite different from those of hard-pressed ordinary people. Why should the dreams of an elite few trump everyone else's?

And, like 'picking winners', the objectives are likely to be chosen on the basis of the 'buzz' around particular social and political issues, not because they serve the needs and purposes of real people. Political realities being what they are, it will be grand, showy and expensive projects that will be chosen over small, targeted and modest ones that might actually deliver more value. If governments really wanted to focus the ingenuity of entrepreneurs on creating human benefit, they might be better to set the right conditions for entrepreneurship and retire.

Lessons from experience

Josh Lerner concludes that the same repeated flaws doom most governments' attempts to boost entrepreneurship. Countries should avoid merely copying what others do, like matching others' business grants and tax subsidies, for example, because those policies are probably misguided too. Even copying what does seem to work elsewhere is likely to fail, because the history, geography, people, culture and markets will be crucially different.

Too local a focus is another common problem. Governments must realise that the venture capital market is international. They need to understand it and move with it, rather than trying to steer public funds into whatever is fashionable or finds their political favour.

Using consultants and financial intermediaries can be an expensive and ineffective strategy too. Often, the bulk of the available government funds end up with the advisors rather than the entrepreneurs they are intended to help.

Tax breaks and subsidies to investors are another common mistake, says Lerner. Their benefit lasts only as long as they do—which, given the changing fortunes of politicians, is generally not very long. Once those incentives expire, investors and entrepreneurs simply look for other locations that promise something similar.

Large up-front tax incentives and subsidies are particularly damaging: they encourage over-expansion and expensive production techniques rather than a focus on what customers really want. An example is the \$120 million that the British government offered the DeLorean Motor Company in the 1970s (more than half of its start-up costs) to produce its famous 'gull wing' model in high-unemployment Northern Ireland. But the demand was not there, the company failed, and both the jobs and the taxpayers' money were lost. Another interesting feature of this case, harking back to the start of this section, is that the UK government felt it had to match or outdo DeLorean's other suitor, the government of Ireland. Trying to match or outdo bad incentives offered by other governments is a certain way to waste a lot of public money to no good effect.

9

The entrepreneurial environment

What, then, can be done more positively in order to boost entrepreneurship and spread its many benefits to society and economic life? A good start might be to look at the institutions of some country that is commonly agreed to be highly entrepreneurial and see what lessons might be drawn from that.

Why is the US so entrepreneurial?

On any measure, the United States is certainly an entrepreneurial country. So, do its institutions give us any clues?

Education? Is a country's education and research strength, perhaps, important in terms of encouraging innovation and entrepreneurship? The US has many of the world's top universities and research institutions. But worldwide, there is no obvious link between entrepreneurship and spending on research.

Market size? Is the size of the local market a factor, with a large domestic market helping entrepreneurs to win customers and expand?

Certainly, the US is a large country, with a population over 325 million. But again, there is no clear link between the size of the home market and entrepreneurship rates. The European Union has an even larger population (445 million), and enjoys free movement of products (and, for the most part, people) between its member states. Nevertheless, on most entrepreneurship measures, it is far less entrepreneurial than the US.

Other factors? Other factors, however, seem much more important. They include access to capital, freedom of innovation and action, culture, taxation, regulation, management quality and the country's legal and other institutions. It is therefore worth looking at these in more detail.

Wealth, freedom and culture

Wealth and capital. The US is rich, with good education and an extensive welfare system. Nearly everyone, therefore, has the educational grounding needed to start a business, and access to the necessary capital from savings, friends and family. Better access to capital may explain a large part of why richer countries tend to be more entrepreneurial (though it could be, conversely, that more entrepreneurial countries tend to generate more wealth).

Freedom. There is also more personal freedom in the US than in most other countries. Does that perhaps give entrepreneurs the ability to experiment with new products and ways of doing business? The statistics certainly suggest that, whatever the reason, freedom and entrepreneurship go together. The countries at the top of the Fraser

Institute's *Economic Freedom of the World* index are also at the top of entrepreneurship measures.[66] There is also a strong correlation (0.87) between countries' freedom scores on the 2019 Heritage Foundation's *Index of Economic Freedom* and their entrepreneurial dynamism as measured by the Legatum Institute *Prosperity Index* Business Environment Pillar score.[67] And there is a strong correlation (0.77) too between countries' overall score in the *Index of Economic Freedom* and their score on the *Global Innovation Index* published by Cornell University, INSEAD and the World Intellectual Property Organization.[68]

"[T]he societies that do the most innovating are the ones with the most freedom for people to exchange ideas. It was freedom, not state direction, that caused both Victorian Britain and modern California to be hotbeds of innovation. It was state dirigisme that prevented Stalin's Russia, Mao's China [and] Mugabe's Zimbabwe...from being similar hotbeds."

—Matt Ridley,

freemarketconservatives.org blog, 24 February 2020

....

66 Kreft, S. and Sobel. R. (2005) 'Public Policy, Entrepreneurship and Freedom.' Washington, D.C.: *The Cato Journal* 25(3): 595-616.

67 Kim, A. (2020) *Economic Freedom: Promoting Economic Opportunity and Prosperity*, presentation to the Mont Pelerin Society, Stanford University, January.

68 *Ibid.*

In other words, it is not just wealth that is important, but freedom too. Around thirty-five countries are richer than Estonia, for example, but it scores highly on measures of both freedom and entrepreneurship.

There are good reasons why this should be so. According to Matt Ridley, the state rarely deserves the credit for sparking innovation. "Far more often," he writes, "inventions and discoveries emerge by serendipity and the exchange of ideas, and are pushed, pulled, moulded, transformed and brought to life by people acting as individuals, firms, markets and yes, sometimes public servants."[69] Innovation is an evolutionary process that works best if people are free to look for new and better ways of doing things.

Openness. An open culture seems to be another important factor. The US, for example, is a welcoming place for entrepreneurs. And Deirdre McCloskey argues that positive attitudes towards business encourages entrepreneurship—and always have. Such 'bourgeois values', she says, explain the expansion of commerce in England before and during the Industrial Revolution; and the same values are alive in the US today.[70] As part of this same US culture, self-improvement is seen as positive, and people are more reluctant to rely on state benefits than they are in many other places. Entrepreneurs and super-entrepreneurs are not vilified, as they are in more socialist countries, but generally admired. And someone's past failures do not exclude them from being taken seriously and trying again.

....

69 Ridley, M. (2020).

70 McCloskey, D. (2007) *The Bourgeois Virtues: Ethics for an Age of Commerce.* University of Chicago Press.

Permissionless innovation

Some legal systems seem to be very much better at encouraging entrepreneurship than others. Entrepreneurship is twice as prevalent in the English legal tradition than the German, for example. Even more remarkable, it is three times greater in the English tradition over the Scandinavian, and five times greater over the French.[71]

Contrasting legal traditions. A possible explanation for these surprising differences is that the English legal tradition was built on common law, which is 'bottom up'. Most decisions are made by the courts, in response to real issues, not by the political authorities in accordance with their own opinions and prejudices. While there are broad principles about what actions are 'reasonable', individuals are generally free to do whatever they want, as long as it does not harm others. That of course is good for innovators. Only if disputes arise—if, say, local residents complain about the litter and congestion caused by 'pop up' food vans in their street—are the courts called on to make a ruling.

Other traditions, deriving from Roman or Napoleonic law, are 'top down' systems. The presumption is that action is permitted only if government authorities specifically permit it. For example, vitamin supplements might do no harm to anyone, but these legal systems may require producers to have specific permission to supply them; and if no rules for this exist, they have to be created. That extra bureaucracy is plainly bad for innovators. And it is harder for new businesses to navigate through thousands of pages of rules than to ensure that their activities meet a few broad principles.

71 Sanandaji, T. and Sanandaji, N. (2014).

Spreading bureaucracy. Indeed, these systems seem to breed yet more (and more detailed) regulatory rules. Regulators themselves would not have a job if they simplified and reduced the burden of red tape. On the contrary, by expanding and deepening it, they can help protect themselves against attack, and demonstrate their diligence and worth. But the growing rule books that these legal systems generate may mean that innovators have to take on an army of regulators even to start up a business, never mind run it. And just as authoritarian government breeds cronyism and corruption, so do such restrictive legal systems breed yet more, and more detailed, regulations and yet more officials.

In addition, many countries increasingly adopt the 'precautionary principle' that it is better to be safe than sorry. Often in response to lobby groups who are worried about, say, the effect of emissions on climate or the potential dangers of genetically modified food, governments impose 'prior restraint' on innovations, putting the onus on entrepreneurs to prove that their innovation is benign. That again does not encourage innovation and risk-taking.

Agenda for growth. By contrast, the more open system of the common-law countries encourages innovation and risk-taking, and it is no surprise that these countries generally lead not just the freedom and ease of doing business league tables but the entrepreneurship and innovation league tables too.

A policy programme to encourage such innovation would build on the bottom-up legal tradition and make 'permissionless innovation' (as the contemporary American economist Adam Thierer calls it) the default. The programme would also remove other barriers to entry and would welcome competition. It would defend free speech and free action, for example. It would rely on principle-driven common law rather than detailed rules, permits and licences. And any restraints on action would be imposed only on the basis of objective costs and benefits.[72]

The importance of taxation

It is questionable whether many of the cultural, moral and legal values mentioned above can be readily transplanted into other countries—though the rapid growth of entrepreneurial businesses in some post-socialist countries may suggest that they can develop anywhere. One thing that might be easier to replicate, however, is the relatively favourable tax and regulatory regime in the US. So important is tax policy to entrepreneurship, it turns out, that lower tax rates alone could explain the high incidence of entrepreneurship in the US.

Because mainstream economics largely ignores or misinterprets entrepreneurship, the mainstream tax policies that derive from such thinking deal poorly with it. At best, they ignore its unique features and needs. At worst, they cripple it.

Tax sensitivity. The textbook view takes firms as given and permanent. It ignores how or why firms come into being, how they grow and develop, why they shut down, and what their different needs are at various stages of their lives. The textbook 'firm' is more like a long-established utility company. The presumption is that the firm invests capital, which generates a predictable reward. If that is so, then tax rates matter little: the textbook firm carries on regardless, passing on any tax rises to its customers and workers in the form of higher prices or lower wages.

72 Thierer, A. (2014).

Real firms, however, are not like that—particularly entrepreneurial firms. They live in an uncertain world. They cannot accurately predict whether their investments will pay off, or not. Countless events—new competition, changing customer demand, supply shortages, management errors—can turn potential future profits into real and present losses. Tax therefore makes a big difference to entrepreneurs' calculations. Taxes on firms, their capital, their supplies, their products, their workers or their customers all raise the risk of losses and failure. Potential entrepreneurs need to be much pickier about their ventures, since they will need to generate higher revenues in order to be reasonably confident of making a return after tax. But revenues and returns are never certain. Consequently, fewer of those potential entrepreneurs will choose to go ahead with their entrepreneurial ventures, and riskier innovations will not happen.

Entrepreneurs list tax as one of the top problems they face. They are much more sensitive to tax rates than are larger firms. Indeed, the Tax Foundation estimates that every 1% rise in US corporation tax leads to a 3.7% fall in the number of new company registrations; while a 10% cut in the income tax rates brings a 12% rise in new hires.[73]

Some countries try to offset this sensitivity, and to encourage small company growth, by taxing capital more than labour, such that taxes bear more heavily on large, capital-intensive firms.[74] But this extra burden can damage innovation within larger firms. And it can damage smaller entrepreneurial enterprises too. Their earnings do not split neatly into income from labour and capital; start-up entrepreneurs'

73 Watson, G. and Kaeding, N. (2019) *Tax Policy and Entrepreneurship: a framework for analysis*. Washington D.C.: Tax Foundation, April 3.

74 Henrekson and Sanandaji (2008).

income is often their capital too, since they use their income to re-invest into the business. So the tax can put a burden on the very thing it wants to promote.

Windfall taxes. The same is true of 'windfall' taxes. Mainstream economic theory holds that, if profits come from accidental good luck, taxing them does not affect companies' behaviour. For instance, when in 2007-08 the price of crude oil soared from $60 to $140 a barrel (mainly due to political turmoil in the Middle East), UK North Sea oil companies made short-term 'windfall profits,' which the British government considered taxing away. Though the price soon fell back and the policy was abandoned, UK Treasury officials thought the tax would be neutral in its effect because it taxed only luck, not enterprise.

But windfall taxes are not neutral. Entrepreneurs know that they can be lucky or unlucky. If they believe that they will bear their bad luck losses but lose their good luck gains, that raises their risk (and, since windfall taxes are arbitrary, their uncertainty) and therefore discourages them from acting entrepreneurially. For example, they may be more reluctant to develop alternative fuels in the hope of profiting from any future political disruption to oil supplies; and the public is denied that choice and security. In addition, even good luck does not come free: a supply problem in one place means that new production needs to be brought online from elsewhere, and distribution networks need to be diverted accordingly. Windfall taxes ignore this extra cost and discourage entrepreneurs from preparing such responses—to the detriment of consumers.

Moreover, the discouragement caused by windfall taxes is much larger for small enterprises than for large ones. Entrepreneurial start-ups may be rich in knowledge and good at spotting opportunities, but they usually have much less capital and liquidity than large firms. While a large firm can therefore absorb unexpected tax bills by selling assets or dipping into reserves, smaller ones may have no saleable assets or spare cash to hand. What capital and cash they have often comes from the entrepreneur's own savings and is immediately re-invested into the business. Moreover, new or small ventures have much less ability to raise finance from banks or shareholders in order to meet unforeseen bills. In addition, it is harder for them to switch their operations into business lines that are less vulnerable to unexpected taxes, as larger firms can: they may have no other lines to expand, and they may not want to do anything else anyway.

Stock option taxes. As we have seen, venture capital plays an important role in turning ideas and start-ups into viable long-term businesses. It is noteworthy that Europe lags behind the US in venture capital activity—and, perhaps as a result, in start-ups and in growing entrepreneurial businesses, even though European financial markets are otherwise strong. One reason might be the different tax treatment of employee stock options.[75]

The risk of failure is high in new and innovative businesses. To manage that risk, venture capital providers often compensate founders and key workers with stock options rather than cash alone. If there are low tax rates on these stock options, that makes investing in entrepreneurial firms more attractive, drawing capital and talent into those sectors and boosting innovation. In the United States, the tax is indeed low because income from employee stock options are treated as

75 Henrekson, M. and Sanandaji, T. (2018) 'Stock option taxation: a missing piece in European innovation policy?' *Small Business Economics*, 51.

capital gains; earnings can be postponed and the tax deferred until the stock is eventually sold. As a result, the US has more venture capital activity than Europe. That in turn increases the likelihood of innovative companies achieving high growth. And then the wider benefits of that entrepreneurial growth are spread through the economy. However, since the entrepreneurial sector is relatively small, such large and general benefits can be achieved at the cost of very little tax foregone by the Treasury.

Other tax problems. Because mainstream economic theory does not take sufficient account of entrepreneurial businesses and their special needs, economic policy designers typically pitch individual and corporate taxes at levels that discourage entrepreneurial risk-taking. Higher (and unpredictable) taxes significantly increase the risks faced by entrepreneurs and reduce the ability of cash-strapped new businesses to afford the talent and equipment they need. They also make it harder for start-ups to access capital. Because of the risks involved, the availability of venture capital is very sensitive to the anticipated investment returns. High and unpredictable taxes reduce those returns and are therefore a major discouragement.

Tax rates that are too high for their job also stimulate avoidance and evasion. This may already be more common in start-ups and smaller firms where accounting standards and financial controls may be less rigorous and less understood. And entrepreneurs, researchers and scientists are mobile. They can avoid overly-high taxes by joining the 'brain drain' and migrating to lower-tax countries. Unfortunately that leaves their home country dry of talent, less dynamic and starved of the benefits of their imagination, effort, innovation and contribution to future economic growth.

The regulatory burden

It is easier to quantify the impact of taxes on enterprises than to quantify the burden of regulation they face. However, there are a few simple measures that might provide some rough indications, such as the time, paperwork and cost of registering a new business. After all, the harder it is to set up a new business, the fewer people will do so. Or they may set up informal businesses that, being outside the law, may be unable to operate very efficiently. For example, their owners may under-invest in premises and equipment, knowing that at any time the (sometimes corrupt) authorities could close them down and confiscate (or steal) their property.

Fortunately, the time that it takes to start a business has fallen from a world average of 50 days in 2003 to less than 20 days now.[76] But there are still large variations. In Venezuela, the figure is 230 days; in the Lao People's Democratic Republic it is 173 days; in Cambodia 99 days. At the other end of the scale, it takes only 4 days to start a business in the US, 2 in Australia, Canada, Hong Kong and Singapore, and just 1 in Georgia and New Zealand. In Estonia, businesses can be established instantly online. Again, there is a clear pattern: starting a business is quick in free and entrepreneurial countries, slow in less free and less entrepreneurial ones. It may also be no coincidence that it is also twice as fast to start a business in high-income countries than it is anywhere else. And higher-income countries, as we have seen, are generally more entrepreneurial ones.

It is harder to measure the financial burden of regulations—or even their number. The *acquis communautaire* (the body of EU's laws and regulations on EU companies, charities and persons) has 35 chapters;

....

76 World Bank Doing Business Project.

officially it is 110,000 pages long and grows at 5,000 pages a year—though nobody seems to know for sure and some estimates put the numbers at twice that. Such large bodies of regulation weigh most heavily on small and start-up businesses, which are less able to comply with them (or even have the time to read and understand them) than larger companies with their experienced compliance departments.

Having too many and too arduous regulations on small businesses encourages corruption. In Nepal, for example, a 2013 survey undertaken by Samriddhi (The Prosperity Foundation) discovered that local shop-keepers had to register with four different government agencies, were monitored by six different agencies, and had to comply with more than 15 specific laws. Unsurprisingly, none of the 268 shops surveyed had all the necessary registrations, often being simply too small to deal with so much regulation. The lack of paperwork makes it difficult for small shop owners to borrow to expand, so their businesses remain inefficiently small. Meanwhile, local police and trading officials routinely threaten to close them down unless they pay a bribe to get the officials to overlook the breach.[77]

Nor is this merely a problem of developing countries. Opening a restaurant in San Francisco, for example, requires 14 different permits, including planning, building, fire, public utilities and others. Some involve considerable time, effort and financial cost. If alcohol is to be served, for example, the intending restaurateur has to mail every resident within 500 feet. Together, these different processes can take nine months to complete, often costing the entrepreneur thousands of dollars in rent on premises that cannot be used until every last permit

77 Samriddhi Foundation (2013) *Economic Freedom Matters: Does Economic Freedom Affect Kirana Pasals in Nepal?*

is signed off by officials.[78]

It is often suggested that reducing regulation will lead to the public getting lower-quality or unsafe products, that monopolies will form or that traders will cynically underpay employees or pollute the environment. Studies suggest that well-designed regulation can indeed improve things on all these fronts and boost economic growth in the process. But they also show that heavily regulated economies have 2%-3% lower economic growth than less heavily regulated ones.[79]

Well-designed regulation is, in any case, the exception, not the rule. Most regulation is driven by political agendas rather than evidence and economic rationality. In addition, larger firms, with their bigger lobbying budgets, have a disproportionate influence on what regulations are adopted. That enables them to protect their businesses against newcomers. The resulting reduction in competition means that customers have to put up with less innovative products, lower quality and higher prices. They also have less ability to boycott companies whom they believe trade unfairly or irresponsibly. And since heavy regulation makes citizens less wealthy, they have less money to spare (after providing the essentials of food, shelter, clothing, utilities and healthcare) on improving environmental standards—switching from cheap coal-fuelled power to more expensive renewable sources, for example. It is only competitive entrepreneurship, through the higher value and economic growth it generates, that enables us to tackle such problems.

78 Tuder, S. (2017) 'What it actually costs to open a restaurant in San Francisco.' *SF Eater*, June 2.

79 Gorgens, T., M. Paldam and A. Würtz (2003) 'How does Public Regulation affect Growth?' *University of Aarhus,* Department of Economics Working Paper No. 2003-14. See also Djankov, S., C. McLeish and R. Ramalho (2006) 'Regulation and Growth.' *World Bank*, Working Paper No. 40722.

The right conditions

Entrepreneurship requires not only the right conditions for entrepreneurs themselves, but the right conditions for their investors, workers and customers too. Entrepreneurs need good access to capital, management skills and advice; they and their customers also need a stable political and economic environment. Only then can people plan and invest for the future in confidence.

Property and justice. There is a positive correlation between the strength and security of property rights in a country and its entrepreneurship rate.[80] Given the uncertainty facing any business, secure property rights and the rule of law are vital to people's decision to risk their money and effort. There is no point in farmers planting a crop, for instance, if they expect that the harvest is likely to be stolen from them at gunpoint.

The need for secure property rights—including copyrights, patents, brands and other 'intellectual' properties—is even greater for entrepreneurs. Most ventures fail, and most entrepreneurial investments do not pay off. So, if people are to take those entrepreneurial risks, they need to be confident that they can reap the reward from the few that succeed.

Nor is it only private greed that property must be protected from. Entrepreneurs are less likely to give up their jobs, start a new business and manage it through to profitability, if they fear that the government itself could arbitrarily tax away the proceeds, close them down for political reasons or allow officials to extract crippling bribes from them. There must be a *rule of law* that treats theft and exploitation

....

80 Sanandaji, T. and Leeson, P. (2013).

by politicians and officials no differently from theft and exploitation by individuals and gangs. And there must be strong and independent justice to back that up. If the justice system is weak or corrupt, people will have little trust in it. Indeed, people will see it as a potentially enormous risk: thieves may steal things from you, but they cannot ban you from trading or throw you in prison. That will leave them very reluctant to make entrepreneurial investments. For the same reasons, political and official power must be limited so that those in power cannot act arbitrarily to exploit others (imposing taxes or confiscating the property of groups who oppose them, for example) and ignore people's individual and civic rights.[81]

Openness. Another important factor is a country's openness to foreign capital and migration. As we have seen, many entrepreneurs are immigrants. They are people who have had the bravery, energy and enterprise to leave their homeland and start afresh somewhere else—all traits that are useful to an entrepreneur. And they are more likely to see opportunities that the locals, bound up in the prevailing culture and imagination, might miss.

Policies to attract (and retain) entrepreneurial immigrants may include work visas for students so that they can study in the host country and stay on to work for a firm in their field of interest. Or even to start their own enterprise: several countries have special visas for foreign entrepreneurs, and even more have special visas granting residence to investors. But an open migration policy that attracts and retains any worker, skilled or not, has a disproportionately high chance of

81 Butler, E. (Forthcoming) *An Introduction to Democracy.* London, Institute of Economic Affairs.

attracting people with entrepreneurial spirit, and, more generally, in promoting prosperity and reducing poverty.[82]

Culture. Institutions such as the legal tradition, the nature and security of property rights, the independence of the judiciary, limits on governments, the defence of rights or the attitudes to migration, are all part of a more general culture of principles, morality and beliefs. It is not easy to reproduce these deep principles in some other culture to which they are foreign.

Nevertheless, the entrepreneurial spirit is strong almost everywhere. Even in the most highly regulated countries, people show remarkable ingenuity in getting around the official rules in order to improve life for themselves and their families. People are hugely resourceful at coping with problems and taking opportunities; their entrepreneurship is quite easily unleashed. So, anything that can be done to unleash it, and turn it from unproductive to productive, can deliver large benefits to the community.

For governments, that means things like understanding the realities of the venture capital market and the special needs of entrepreneurs; leveraging education and research; being open to migrants and to foreign capital; taking a long-term view rather than attempting quick fixes; not over-engineering support programmes; avoiding upfront subsidies and tax breaks; being wary of consultants; and avoiding the mistakes of others.

....

82 Caplan, B. (Forthcoming) *Poverty—Who's to Blame?*

The importance of management[83]

Such an approach may boost creativity, ideas generation, innovation and risk-taking. However, to turn ideas into profitable business, entrepreneurs need technical skills and organisational abilities too.[84]

Firms can succeed or fail for a variety of reasons (Paul Graham identifies 18 different reasons for failure)[85] but good or bad management is a particularly important one. Often entrepreneurs struggle with the mechanics of running a business, controlling costs, adjusting to rapid growth or getting to customers. Turning good ideas into commercial success requires good management.

Managers themselves are, in a sense, entrepreneurial. For example, they might work out innovative ways to increase customer satisfaction, so that people believe they are getting even better value from the entrepreneur's product. They might find ways to make old and undervalued products more attractive or more useful. And just as entrepreneurs combine productive resources in new ways to create better or cheaper products, so do managers combine human resources to make those products more appealing to customers.

The large gap between the most and the least productive firms might have many causes—not just low interest rates keeping 'zombie' firms alive, but possibly regulation, weak competition or poor education. Much of the gap, however, might be attributable to the quality of

....

83 Dumitriu, S. (2019) *Management Matters.* London: The Entrepreneurs Network, January 23.

84 Ward, T. (2005) 'An Integrated Model of Entrepreneurship and Intrapreneurship.' Paper delivered to the 13th Annual High Technology Small Firms Conference.

85 Graham, P. (2005) 'The 18 Mistakes that Kill Startups.'

management in different businesses. The best firms monitor their business and try to improve performance, promoting the things and the people that succeed best and fixing failure when they find it. The least productive firms do not.[86]

Given the potential rewards of good management, it is surprising that good practice does not necessarily spread. But under-performing firms might not even realise that they are getting things wrong. Perhaps poor performers are so focused on the core tasks of production that they do not have time to think about the wider management issues. Perhaps they cannot imagine what aspects of their operation could be easily improved. They may lack the motivation to do things differently, or fear change. They may try to implement reforms but struggle to make them work.

"Entrepreneurial management in the new venture has four requirements: It requires, first, a focus on the market. It requires, second, financial foresight, and especially planning for cash flow and capital needs ahead. It requires, third, building a top management team long before the new venture actually needs one and long before it can actually afford one. And finally, it requires of the founding entrepreneur a decision in respect to his or her own role, area of work, and relationships."

—Peter F. Drucker, *Innovation and Entrepreneurship*

....

86 Dumitriu, S. (2019) *Management Matters.*

The Entrepreneurs Network, a UK think-tank, notes that in India, simply giving small firms free management advice raised management productivity by 11%.[87] Arguably the most effective thing that a government can do in order to boost the success of entrepreneurs, therefore, may be to ensure they have access to such advice. The Network also suggests that governments should try to help entrepreneurs identify the best management ideas by promoting trials of different management training systems and techniques. They should also allow or encourage firms to invest in upgrading their management capabilities, perhaps through apprenticeship. Peer-to-peer networks to share good practice are also important: through this technique China increased firms' revenues by 8%, boosting profitability and the productivity of managers.

The lessons

Certainly, we should care about boosting entrepreneurship for all the reasons given at the start of this book; and government may have a role in that. But it should be 'tough' love, not a stream of tax concessions, subsidies, grants and other giveaways, says the Network. Though entrepreneurs often complain of being short of funds, so does everyone: finance is not the biggest barrier to starting up a business, which usually does not take a great deal of capital. Government finance, however, encourages the creation of overblown ventures that are fundamentally unviable and makes entrepreneurs over-optimistic. The best and most durable businesses are not 'made' but evolve and grow naturally from small start-ups, following the demands of their customers.

87 *Ibid.*

Another common idea is that governments must improve education, training and skills. Certainly, all those things help create and nourish entrepreneurial firms. But they do not have to be *provided* by government, which tends to deliver them in a very bureaucratic way that may not be in tune with market needs. Entrepreneurs do not need civil-service-run training programmes. People learn more about business at work than they ever could in classrooms or training colleges. And entrepreneurs know who to train in what way and for what purpose better than distant officials. Instead of offering training, governments need to *allow* people to cultivate their own human capital. That might mean structuring the tax system to support training and human capital development.

Liberalisation of trade and commerce, and an open, competitive business environment are also crucial to the spread and success of entrepreneurship. Again, that does not require government to set up small-business bureaucracies. It requires them to remove barriers to international trade, welcome migrants, end discrimination against women and minorities who may bring new ideas into business, simplify employment laws, taxes, social charges and licencing, and much more—especially for smaller firms whom they impact the most. And it means tackling monopolies (especially state monopolies) and reducing the barriers to entering or creating new markets.

When Alexander the Great met the Cynic philosopher Diogenes (who eschewed worldly comforts and lived in a barrel), he asked: "Great Diogenes, what can I, with all my wealth and armies, do for you?" Diogenes looked up at him and waved him away, saying: "Just stand out of the sun." If governments really want entrepreneurship and its benefits to grow, standing out of their sunlight seems sound advice.

FURTHER READING

Block, J. *Corporate Income Taxes and Entrepreneurship.* IZA World of Labor. https://wol.iza.org/articles/corporate-income-taxes-and-entrepreneurship

Decker, R. A., Haltiwanger, J., Jarmin, R. S. and Miranda J.(2016) 'Declining Business Dynamism: Implications for Productivity?' *Brookings Institution*, Hutchins Centre Working Paper No. 23, September 19. https://www.brookings.edu/research/declining-business-dynamism-implications-for-productivity/

Dumitriu, S. (2019) 'Management Matters.' *The Entrepreneurs Network*, January 23. https://www.tenentrepreneurs.org/research/management-matters

Dumitriu, S. and Stewart, A. (2019) 'Job Creators: The Immigrant Founders of Britain's Fastest Growing Companies.' *The Entrepreneurs Network.* https://www.tenentrepreneurs.org/immigrantfounders

Foss, N. and Klein, P. (2010) 'Alertness, Action, and the Antecedents of Entrepreneurship.' In *The Journal of Private Enterprise* 25(2): 145-164. https://organizationsandmarkets.files.wordpress.com/2010/07/fk_jope_2010.pdf

Global Entrepreneurship Monitor (2019) '2018/2019 Global Report.' *Global Entrepreneurship Research Association*, London Business School. https://www.gemconsortium.org

Hathaway, I. and Litan, R. (2014) 'What's Driving the Decline in the Firm Formation Rate? A Partial Explanation.' Brookings Institution. Brookings Economic Studies, November. https://www.brookings.edu/wp-content/uploads/2016/06/driving_decline_firm_formation_rate_hathaway_litan.pdf

Henrekson, M. and Sanandaji, T. (2008) 'Entrepreneurship and the Theory of Taxation.' *Research Institute of Industrial Economics*, IFN Working Paper No. 732. SSRN-id1089367.pdf

Henrekson, M. and Sanandaji, T. (2011) 'The Interaction of Entrepreneurship and Institutions.' In *Journal of Institutional Economics* 7(1): 47-75. https://www.cambridge.org/core/journals/journal-of-institutional-economics/article/interaction-of-entrepreneurship-and-institutions/DD9AF1A1BFA6DC0714066B09E9D52E0C

Henrekson, M. and Sanandaji, T. (2014) 'Small Business Activity Does Not Measure Entrepreneurship.' In *Proceedings of the National Academy of Sciences of the United States of America*, 111(5): 1760-1765. https://www.pnas.org/content/111/5/1760.short

Henrekson, M. (2020) 'How Labor Market Institutions affect Job Creation and Productivity Growth.' *IZA World of Labor*, 38. https://wol.iza.org/articles/how-labor-market-institutions-affect-job-creation-and-productivity-growth/long

Kritikos, A. (2014) 'Entrepreneurs and their Impact on Jobs and Economic Growth'. *IZA World of Labor,* 8. https://wol.iza.org/articles/entrepreneurs-and-their-impact-on-jobs-and-economic-growth

Klein, D. (2009) Chapter 9: 'Let's be Pluralist on Entrepreneurship.' In *Knowledge and Coordination: A Liberal Interpretation*. Oxford, UK: Oxford University Press. https://www.oxfordscholarship.com/view/10.1093/acprof:osobl/9780199355327.001.0001/acprof-9780199355327-chapter-9

Klein, P. (2017) 'Why Government Cannot Be Run Like a Business.' *Mises Institute,* Mises Wire, September 4.https://mises.org/wire/why-government-cannot-be-run-business

Klein, P. and Foss, N. (2014) 'The Right Way to View Entrepreneurship.' *Mises Institute,* Mises Daily Articles, July 19. https://mises.org/library/right-way-view-entrepreneurship

Klein, P. and Mariotti, S. (2013) 'Looking at Entrepreneurship from a Theoretical Perspective, with Leading Expert Peter Klein.' *HuffPost*, December 30. https://www.huffpost.com/entry/looking-at-entrepreneursh_b_4505632?_guc_consent_skip=1581182929&guccounter=1

McMaken, R. (2014) 'Extended Version of Peter Klein's Interview on Entrepreneurship.' *Mises Institute*, Mises Wire Interview Transcription, April 8. https://mises.org/wire/extended-version-peter-kleins-interview-entrepreneurship

Lofstrom, M. and Wang, C. (2019) 'Immigrants and Entrepreneurship.' *IZA World of Labor*, 85. https://wol.iza.org/subject-areas/entrepreneurship

Lerner, J. (2009) *Boulevard of Broken Dreams: Why Public Efforts to Boost Entrepreneurship and Venture Capital Have Failed—and What to Do About It.* Princeton University Press. https://press.princeton.edu/books/paperback/9780691154534/boulevard-of-broken-dreams

Masnik, M. (2017) 'The Dangerous Rise of Unproductive Entrepreneurship.' *Techdirt*, August 18. https://www.techdirt.com/articles/20170818/00183838020/dangerous-rise-unproductive-entrepreneurship.shtml

McCloskey, D. (2007) *The Bourgeois Virtues: Ethics for an Age of Commerce*. University of Chicago Press.

Medairos, J. and Mazzucato, M. (2019) 'This Economist has a Plan to Fix Capitalism. It's Time we all Listened.' *Wired*, October 8. https://www.wired.co.uk/article/mariana-mazzucato

Nanda, R. (2016) *Financing High-Potential Entrepreneurship.* IZA World of Labor. https://wol.iza.org/articles/financing-high-potential-entrepreneurship

Ridley, M. (2020) *How Innovation Works.* Fourth Estate.

Sanandaji, T. and Leeson, P. (2013) Billionaires. *Industrial and Corporate Change*, 22(1): 313–337. https://academic.oup.com/icc/article/22/1/313/885637

Sanandaji, T. and Sanandaji, N. (2014) 'SuperEntrepreneurs—And how your country can get them.' Centre for Policy Studies. https://www.cps.org.uk/research/superentrepreneurs-and-how-your-country-can-get-them/

Schaeffer, V. (2015) 'Corporate Entrepreneurship and Creativity in Large Firms: The Practice of Start-up Contests.' In *Journal of Innovation Economics & Management,* 3(18): 25-51. https://www.cairn.info/revue-journal-of-innovation-economics-2015-3-page-25.htm#

Seth, S (2019) 'Why Entrepreneurship Is Important to the Economy.' *Investopedia*, July 22. https://www.investopedia.com/articles/personal-finance/101414/why-entrepreneurs-are-important-economy.asp

Thierer, A. (2014) *Permissionless Innovation: The Continuing Case for Comprehensive Technological Freedom.* Arlington Virginia: Mercatus Center at George Mason University.

Vaz-Curado, S. and Mueller, A. (2019) 'The Concept of Entrepreneur of Schumpeter in Comparison to Kirzner.' In *Mises Interdisciplinary Journal of Philosophy Law and Economics* 7(3). https://www.revistamises.org.br/misesjournal/article/view/1223/656

Watson, G. and Kaeding, N. (2019) 'Tax Policy and Entrepreneurship: A Framework for Analysis.' Washington, D.C.: Tax Foundation, April 3. https://taxfoundation.org/tax-policy-entrepreneurship/

About the Author

Eamonn Butler is Director of the Adam Smith Institute, a leading think tank in the UK. He holds degrees in economics and psychology, a PhD in philosophy, and an honorary DLitt. A former winner of the Freedom Medal of Freedom's Foundation at Valley Forge and the UK National Free Enterprise Award, Eamonn is currently Secretary of the Mont Pelerin Society. Butler is the author of many books, including introductions on the pioneering economists Adam Smith, Milton Friedman, F. A. Hayek, and Ludwig von Mises. He has also published primers on Classical Liberalism, Public Choice, Magna Carta, the Austrian School of Economics, and great liberal thinkers, as well as *The Condensed Wealth of Nations* and *The Best Book on the Market*. His *Foundations of a Free Society* won the 2014 Fisher Prize.

About AIER

The American Institute for Economic Research in Great Barrington, Massachusetts, was founded in 1933 as the first independent voice for sound economics in the United States. Today it publishes ongoing research, hosts educational programs, publishes books, sponsors interns and scholars, and is home to the world-renowned Bastiat Society and the highly respected Sound Money Project. The American Institute for Economic Research is a 501c3 public charity.

About the IEA

This book is a co-production between the American Institute for Economic Affairs and the Institute of Economic Affairs (IEA).

The Institute is a research and educational charity (No. CC 235 351), limited by guarantee. Its mission is to improve understanding of the fundamental institutions of a free society by analysing and expouding the role of markets in solving economic and social problems.

The IEA, which was established in 1955 by the late Sir Antony Fisher, is an educational charity, not a political organisation. It is independent of any political party or group and does not carry on activities intended to affect support for any political party or candidate in any election or referendum, or at any other time. It is financed by sales of publications, conference fees and voluntary donations.

In addtion to its main series of publications, the IEA also publishes (jointly with the University of Buckingham), *Economic Affairs*.

IEA publications enjoy widespread classroom use and course adoptions in schools and universities. They are also sold throughout the world and often translated/reprinted.

Since 1974 the IEA has helped to create a worldwide network of 100 similar institutions in over 70 countries. They are all independent but share the IEA's mission.

INDEX

Printed in Great Britain
by Amazon

68920392R00087